D1391986

Middlesbrough College
00101674

# Praise for *The Perfect Maths Lesson*

As someone who struggled with maths growing up, I often asked/wailed, 'Why *are* we learning this?' Ian understands the need to bring the real world into the classroom, to give maths value and to engage learners so that they have a reason to show up. He provides pupils with stimulating real-life contexts that will challenge and prepare them, not make-believe contexts used simply to practise strategies or pass a test. Therefore, young people can adapt to our 'compressed global community' whilst becoming better learners; they are learning to learn in maths to empower them for the future.

So, why should you read this book? Like any good teacher, regardless of subject area, Ian knows you have to hook pupils in and challenge them from the off, but then maintain this pace and balance throughout the lesson: he summarises how to do this with top tips. I will be keeping this book to hand as a gentle reminder and to try out some of his practical ideas and activities (from starters to original and creative assessment opportunities) to 'perplex, mystify and delightfully baffle' learners, which he succeeded in doing to this reader many times. He even includes mathematical jokes and inspirational sayings, as he knows that learning for children is emotional and they have to enjoy it.

His handy checklists guide you through the whole process of the planning, delivery and assessment of an outstanding lesson, with references to Ofsted's expectations, although the learners are the main concern, first and foremost. There are even novel ways of setting homework which promote real independent learning (not just working on your own) and the discipline for students to push themselves.

Ian continually endorses challenge, 'occupying a space at the edge of their ability', so young people embrace being stuck and see it as 'an exciting gateway' to new knowledge or skills. Children's fear of failure is bigger in maths so he illustrates how to encourage them to 'fail better'. They will then feel more able to take risks in these real-life/unknown situations, as the children's emotional well-being is at the heart of his drive to make maths fun and accessible for all.

In my classroom, I will now be posing, pausing, pouncing and bouncing with my pupils to ensure they truly understand maths and are not merely 'doing' it, and so that I am teaching with students not to them.

**Ruth Saxton, primary teacher and Chair of the National Association for the Teaching of Drama**

*The Perfect Maths Lesson* is a concise guide to teaching maths and is full of interesting pedagogy and practical ideas. Whilst regularly referencing Ofsted, the mathematical learning that children undertake remains the focal point, as it should. Ian Loynd's enthusiasm for the subject, and for teaching, comes across in abundance and all readers should close the back cover having taken away new ideas to implement in the classroom.

**Oliver Saunders, maths teacher, Millfield School**

*The Perfect Maths Lesson* will be a great addition to the 'Perfect family' of books in our staffroom library. This little book contains a wealth of good ideas, all of which can be modified and extended to use across different age ranges. It is a good mix of practical ideas to try in lessons and theory to improve teaching and learning. I found it really easy to read and it even made me smile in places. As always, the checklists at the end of each chapter will help teachers to reflect on their classroom practice; this will definitely lead to a better experience for children in our school. I particularly enjoyed the cheesy mathematical jokes and will definitely be trying them out on my children! Thank you.

**Beverley Dandy, Head Teacher, Outwoods Primary School**

This is my first experience of the 'Perfect Lesson' series from Jackie Beere and friends and, to me, the title has a lot to live up to! I needn't have worried. From the start, Ian gives compelling and motivating reasons for learning; not just learning maths, but any learning and, particularly importantly, advises on how to deal with the ultimate question, 'Why are we learning this?' He frames the learning and content of the book within the context of the modern, 'flat' world, which every conscientious teacher is desperately trying to give their learners an advantage in. Now I'm hooked.

I read the rest of the book with enthusiasm, even though it is about maths! Ian delivers an excellent balance of theory and context with hundreds (well, it seemed like hundreds; I haven't actually counted them) of practical examples that any teacher can take into a classroom tomorrow. From engaging and challenging learners, including some great ideas for using apparatus through to chilli heat-rated activities to increase independence, the wealth of thought-provoking exercises makes this book a must-have in any staffroom. There is a hugely important chapter on emotional connections with learners and the end-of-chapter checklists act as quick reminders and useful pointers.

So, will this book mean you deliver the perfect maths lesson? Personally, I don't think any book, no matter how good, can; but this one will provide you with a whole toolbox of strategies and ideas that cannot fail to improve the learning in your lessons. And here's the important bit: any learning could be improved by using this book. The underlying principles, with a bit of un-maths tweaking, will have a direct impact on your teaching and, although the book has a secondary 'flavour', these can be equally applied to the primary phase.

In sum-mary (I tried really hard to resist a number of maths puns!), if you're looking for easily accessible ideas and strategies to refresh your teaching, whether in maths or other curriculum areas, this book will be an excellent addition to your collection. It's a quick and easy read that you can dive into at any point and pull out a gem. And, who knows, maybe that will be the one that secures the 'outstanding' judgement – or better still, gives your learners an advantage in the real world!

Now, I'm off to look at the rest of the 'Perfect Lesson' series!

**Paul Bannister, Head Teacher, Highbank Primary School**

# THE PERFECT MATHS LESSON

Totally Practical

Ian Loynd Edited by Jackie Beere

Independent Thinking Press

First published by
Independent Thinking Press
Crown Buildings, Bancyfelin, Carmarthen, Wales, SA33 5ND, UK
www.independentthinkingpress.com

Independent Thinking Press is an imprint of Crown House Publishing Ltd.



First published 2014. Reprinted 2014.



**British Library Cataloguing-in-Publication Data**
A catalogue entry for this book is available
from the British Library.

**Print ISBN 978-178135137-6**
**Mobi ISBN 978-17815199-4**
**ePub ISBN 978-178135200-7**
**ePDF ISBN 978-178135201-4**

Printed and bound in the UK by
Gomer Press, Llandysul, Ceredigion

For Greg

# Contents

# Acknowledgements

To the wonderfully talented, exceptionally dedicated and invariably barmy colleagues I have had the pleasure of working alongside over the last decade. These ideas are entirely yours, unashamedly stolen, tried, tested and summarised neatly in this little book. To my family, who have encouraged me, supported me and reminded me that there is more to life than school. To Jackie, for her expert guidance. To Caroline and Crown House Publishing for having confidence in me. And to all the young people who make my job the best in the world. Thank you.

# Foreword

I have trained teachers for a couple of decades now, but I always know that my biggest challenge is to ensure that the maths teachers feel that what I am saying and doing is relevant for their subject. They are some of the most scrutinised and pressurised teachers in schools and often feel that the unique demands of their subject make it difficult to apply some aspects of research on teaching and learning to their classroom practice. As an English teacher myself, I am in awe of how great maths teachers excite and engage their students, and on many occasions I have observed maths lessons and learned something new.

So, let's be clear: being a maths teacher is a tough job. Furthermore, we have a shortage of maths teachers who are able to really engage and inspire young people to love the subject. We are constantly told that the quality of maths education in the UK is not good enough when judged against international standards, so it is hardly surprising that maths teachers can sometimes feel maligned or even cynical about their job.

This book is an antidote to all of the above.

Ian's love for maths and his ability to apply his knowledge of the way learning works in a maths classroom shines out so much that I feel like I want to go and sit in his lessons on a rainy Friday afternoon and learn algebra. His passion for practical solutions that stimulate engagement and interest provide maths teachers with a range of ideas that can be used immediately.

Important guidance on the craft of maths teaching comes through in examples of questioning and feedback that clarify how a teacher can truly become John Hattie's 'change agent'. The focus on creating emotionally intelligent classrooms where children love learning challenges is particularly relevant as too many students find learning maths scary or just plain boring.

This book is not just for maths teachers – it's for anyone interested in teaching and learning because it gives such an insight into the 'how to do it' (and why it works) of outstanding lessons. It has been thoroughly researched against the national frameworks for inspection and the latest innovative thinking in education, and it provides a plethora of ideas and solutions that all teachers will find useful, whatever the stage of their career. Ian's belief in flexible, child-centred approaches to teaching permeate his philosophy, while his record as a highly successful maths teacher and school leader proves that these strategies work.

*The Perfect Maths Lesson* has that special combination of passion and pragmatism that makes it an immensely welcome addition to the Perfect series – enjoy!

Jackie Beere, Tiffield

# Introduction

Delivering the perfect maths lesson is no simple task. My aim in this book is to provide practical ideas and common-sense methods that can help every teacher to be excellent, and uncover the essential strategies that help teachers appear to walk on water (or at least secure an 'outstanding' judgement)!

## The 'perfect' maths lesson?

Teachers have the most important job in the world. At a time when expectations and accountability are at an all-time high, delivering excellence in the classroom has never been more difficult. The perfect maths lesson is about getting it right for inspectors by first getting it right for the children you teach. This book aims to be a pragmatic and down-to-earth guide, recognising that, although no teacher is perfect, their lessons can be. It is about learning and teaching as much as it is about surviving that dreaded lesson observation.

Jackie Beere (2012b) has provided us with a concise overview of the elements of the perfect (Ofsted) lesson. This book builds on her insights but is written with maths teachers and maths lessons in mind. But, like hers, much of this book can (and should) be applied in all areas of the curriculum. It is not designed to be a mechanistic checklist of expectations which inspectors will tick for compliance. Instead, *The Perfect Maths Lesson* explores the common features of outstanding maths lessons and the characteristics and habits of outstanding maths teachers. You'll find plenty of Ofsted guidance referenced throughout this book, but bear in mind that this advice has been selected because it is good for children and useful for teachers. Great teachers know what works well for their students despite what Ofsted, or anybody else, has to say on the matter. After all, teachers are not in it for the income; they are in it for the outcome.

Ask any parent or child which subject is the most important at school and we can be confident that maths will feature towards the top of the list. It is true that numeracy (like literacy) is an essential skill for effective participation in the 'real' world, and that, nationally, higher levels of numeracy and literacy are closely associated with market success (see e.g. Chiswick et al., 2003). But placing maths at the top of a hierarchy of school subjects is not necessarily good for maths education. The best learners are inquisitive and curious; they are willing to take risks and think for themselves. Yet too many talented and brilliant children believe that they are incapable because the things they are good at are not valued as highly as the ability to solve equations or simplify fractions. This book aims to help teachers nurture creativity, talent and skill by examining how we can develop the essential elements of outstanding maths education so that children learn to appreciate and love maths.

> It remains a concern that secondary pupils seemed so readily to accept the view that learning mathematics is important but dull. They frequently told inspectors that in other subjects they enjoyed regular collaboration on tasks in pairs or groups and discussion of their ideas, yet they often did not do so in their mathematics lessons, or even expect to do so.
>
> Ofsted (2012a: 19)

If you are looking for ideas to breathe new life into your lessons or tops tips to gain that elusive 'outstanding' judgement, you'll find plenty in this book. However, becoming a teacher of the perfect maths lesson requires consistent effort and an unwavering commitment to the people that matter most: the children we teach.

## Why are we learning this?

It's a good question, isn't it? Yet too often I have found myself unable to provide a credible answer to students (at least one that I believed, anyway). Why *am* I teaching this to my class? Am I being constrained by schemes of work, portfolios of evidence, tests and examinations? Do I plan learning episodes based on chapters of the textbook instead of the interests, needs and values of my students? *The Perfect Maths Lesson* is the result of the resistance, revolution and liberation of both teacher and learner that allows mathematics to be enjoyed, explored and understood (and, at the same time, ensures 'good' grades).

Feelings of frustration, such as these, are commonplace in maths education. Maths teachers have long struggled to do both what is right for children and their learning and also what is necessary to 'produce the goods' when it comes to exams. As Ofsted has said:

> In discussion with inspectors, although most secondary teachers recognised the importance of pedagogic skills in mathematics, they often commented on the pressures of external assessments on them and their pupils. Feeling constrained by these pressures and by time, many concentrated on approaches they believed prepared pupils for tests and examinations, in effect, 'teaching to the test'. This practice is widespread and is a significant barrier to improvement.
>
> Ofsted (2008a: 44)

Rethinking maths education in an interdependent and interconnected world is essential if we are to successfully prepare students to live, work and lead in the world. After all, whilst our thinking as teachers is typically developed in a local context, students will be increasingly shaped in their adult lives by global factors. The erudite and provocative author Daniel Pink (2005: 307) tells us that if students are to secure jobs which are 'untouchable' (that is, jobs which a computer cannot do faster or a talented foreigner do cheaper and just as well) then lessons must focus more on creativity, pattern recognition, inventiveness and 'big picture' thinking. And, by cultivating these cross-cultural skills, maths teachers will help children to become competent participants in a globalised world.

Modern maths is addressing the opportunities, dilemmas and conundrums of a compressed global community, and maths teachers need to bring the real world into the classroom to engage learners. Why are we learning this? We are learning this because somebody needs to prevent heart disease and improve online security – *and it could be you*. We are learning this so that we can keep our trains running on time and enhance the performance of Formula 1 cars. We are learning this to predict climate change, preserve our coastlines and make oceanographic forecasts. We are learning this to increase the safety of our military's frontline, to fight viruses and to contribute to the digital arts. We are learning this so that you can change the world – so let's get on with our lesson, shall we?

> At some stage, most teachers are asked questions by pupils about the usefulness of what is being taught. Many feel uncomfortable with these, especially with more abstract concepts, often resorting to answering, 'It's on the syllabus'. Few talk about specific applications or explain the power of being able to think mathematically.
>
> Ofsted (2008a: 41)

The UK system of education has increasingly given credence to international testing as a measure of school effectiveness. The OECD Programme for International Student Assessment (PISA) is a global study which has won particular favour with governments and has been used to berate the performance of British schools over the last two decades as at best stagnant and at worst declining (see e.g. Coughlan, 2013). However, such assessments do little to tell the 'whole story'. What we do know is that high scores in international assessments have no bearing on national measures of wealth, economic growth, productivity or quality of life (see Baker, 2007: 103). In fact, high international test scores can come at the expense of entrepreneurial and creative capacity. Therefore an education system that places an emphasis on testing (and, ergo, the best schools being those that get the best grades) is likely to neglect the type of authentic learning that could make a difference to a country's global competiveness.

As routine jobs are increasingly outsourced to cheaper labour markets, an economic advantage will be gained by students who are able to solve problems, develop flexible new disciplines and have advanced communication skills. Three-time Pulitzer Prize winner Thomas Friedman (2006) has determined that, in his 'flat' world, the most important ability students can develop is the ability to 'learn how to learn'. He argues that, in a world in which digitisation, automation and outsourcing of jobs leads to rapid changes in industry, it is not only what you know but how you learn that will provide an advantage. Metacognition (that is, thinking about thinking) is an important skill that students must develop if they are to be adaptable in the global community. Put simply, learners must think about their own thinking so as to control and change how they learn (or, as Jackie Beere (2013: 9) describes it, 'thinking on purpose').

So, why *are* we learning this?

Because it's relevant, not because it's next in the textbook.

Because it teaches us creativity, pattern recognition, inventiveness and 'big picture' thinking, not because it's in the scheme of work.

Because it helps us to solve problems and be flexible, not because it's on the test.

Because it gives us the skills we need to participate successfully in the world, not because we all need algebra when we're adults.

Because it will grow our brains and make us brave learners, not because it's a 'core' subject.

Because it's fun (or, at least, my teacher makes it feel fun).

# Chapter 1
# Engaging Learners in Maths Lessons

Engaging learners in their learning is an essential element of the perfect maths lesson. Students who are engaged in the learning process are more likely to maintain focus and attention, are more ambitious in their thinking and are more resilient when making mistakes along the way. This is because they are intrinsically motivated to learn, meaning that students derive pleasure from participation in the mathematical task itself, from the challenge it presents or from finding its solution. The best maths lessons are the ones during which pupils acquire new skills and knowledge – and love every moment of it!

> [In outstanding lessons] teachers and other adults authoritatively impart knowledge to ensure students are engaged in learning, and generate high levels of commitment to learning across the school.
>
> Ofsted (2014: 39)

One of the key tasks in engaging learners in maths lessons is to set the pace of the learning correctly. A well-paced lesson enables students to tackle difficult concepts without feeling overwhelmed and maintains momentum through easier tasks before boredom sets in. The *pace* of learning is very different to the *speed* at which the lesson moves. In the best maths lessons, teachers do not try to cram too much in and nor do they take too long to get to the main activity. Instead, the pace of the lesson reflects the ability of the learners in the class and the level of mathematics being studied.

The correct pace allows learners to learn without becoming frustrated (your lesson is too easy, too slow or too repetitive) or becoming bewildered (your lesson is too difficult, too fast or too busy). An effective pace is fast enough to maintain focus but not so fast that students become disconnected from the learning. It is slow enough to ensure understanding but not so slow that students become disinterested.

When planning maths lessons, it is useful to think about the following questions:

- Does the pace of this lesson vary with each learning episode?
- Is there a short, snappy activity to set the scene and 'hook' learners into the learning?
- Is there room for reflection and for asking questions? Will the lesson benefit from a gentler pace as the challenge increases?

- Are there long periods of static, stationary learning that need to be broken up with movement or a change in pace?
- How will I use time limits to keep learning focused?
- Are my resources prepared? How will they be deployed without sabotaging the pace of the lesson?
- Does this lesson involve me talking too much?

Another powerful strategy for engaging learners is to link learning to students' lives. In the perfect maths lesson, students are engaged by solving real-world problems in practical and experimental ways. This might involve planning a holiday, comparing mobile telephone tariffs, plotting routes on a map, breaking a code or monitoring the school's energy consumption. For example, consider how you might build a lesson (or series of lessons) around the following scenarios:

- Imagine two different mobile phone tariffs: the first is a pay-as-you-go tariff and calls cost 35p per minute; the second is a rental contract with a monthly fee of £10 and calls cost 15p per minute. Which tariff gives the best deal?[1]
- Calculate the cost of repainting your classroom walls with two coats of paint.

1 This idea was inspired by Teachers TV: Maths KS3: Mobile Phone Tariffs. Available at: <http://www.tes.co.uk/teaching-resource/Teachers-TV-Maths-KS3-Mobile-Phone-Tariffs-6085220>.

- Conduct a frequency analysis of the following Caesar shift cipher to break the code and reveal the hidden message: AOL WLYMLJA THAOZ SLZZVU.[2]
- You have won a holiday to a destination of your choice! Plan your dream holiday, including all costs, within a budget of £3,000.

> Outstanding learning in mathematics is only possible when pupils and teachers are creative in lessons and see mathematics as a necessary part of their lives. [Head teacher Derek Brooks] says: 'There needs to be a passion for getting inside the key ideas ... pupils need to see that mathematics is something that can be argued about and grappled with. This means that we needed to remove some of the traditional constraints that we know can deliver consistently good and better lessons, and allow teachers to take risks.'
>
> Ofsted (2012c: 1)

Maths teachers need to be cautious, however, and use contexts sensibly and responsibly. Make-believe contexts, used over time, which do not genuinely draw on pupils' real-world knowledge, restrict children's interest in maths. As the internet meme asserts, 'Maths: The only place where people buy 60 watermelons and nobody wonders why'. Make-believe

2 See <http://www.simonsingh.net/The_Black_Chamber/caesar.html> for a whistle-stop tour of the world of cryptography. For even more fun, try making Code Wheels with your pupils – see McFall (2013: 158–159).

contexts will, at best, make maths appear less relevant than other subjects at school and, at worst, will lead to children ignoring contexts altogether, leading to mistakes in their understanding.[3] One thing that is sure to capture the imagination of any maths class, however, is a good mystery to solve! For example:

> *Good morning Year 7. Take your seats quickly and quietly, thank you. Something serious is afoot and I need your help. This is an urgent matter! The school is experiencing a sequence of burglaries and the head teacher has asked for your assistance in bringing those responsible to justice. On Monday, Mr Jones in room 1 found that his dictionary had been stolen. On Tuesday, Mrs Davies in room 2 discovered that her oil paints were missing. On Wednesday, Miss Edwards in room 4 noticed that her metronome had been taken. Today is Thursday. You must determine where our thief will strike next so that we can catch them in the act!*

This introduction to sequences is certain to engage learners as they compete to be the first to convince the teacher that they hold the key to solving this crime. Perhaps room 7 is next to be targeted? Possibly room 8? Extend learning by considering where the thief will strike on Friday. Rooms 11, 12 and 16 are now all contenders, which can lead to detailed dialogue about common ratios, indices, quadratics, Fibonacci and more. Moreover, a little 'friendly controversy' will hold

---

3 According to Boaler (2009: 45), children will, over time, learn that to succeed in 'mathsland' you must leave your common sense at the classroom door!

learners' attention as they discuss, debate and critically evaluate one another's possible solutions.[4]

Getting the perfect maths lesson off to the right start is crucial to engaging learners. An effective initial activity sets the tone for the rest of the learning and can determine the success (or otherwise) of the lesson. Your pupils need to be in the habit of beginning their learning as soon as they walk through the door of your classroom. As they wait for others to arrive, it is a good idea to have a little, open-ended challenge available on the board or on their table. For example:

- How many ways are there to make 10 pence using British coins?[5]
- How many days/hours/minutes are left until the end of term?
- How many triangles are there in this diagram?[6]

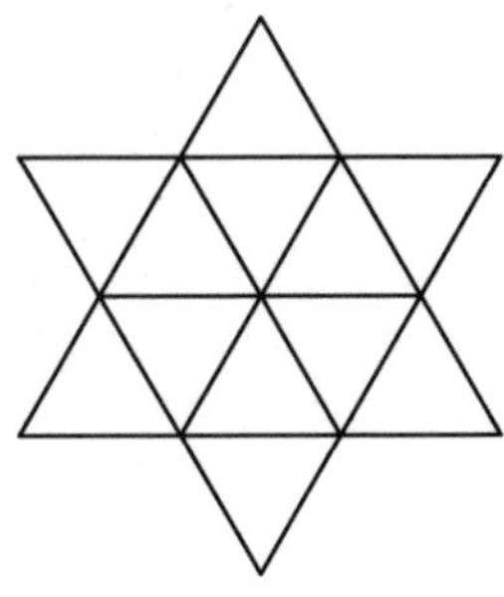

4 See Gary Rimmer's *Number Freaking* (2006) for a cheerfully absurd collection of surreal everyday arithmetic.

5 There are 11.

6 There are 20.

Tackling a fun initial challenge individually or in pairs as soon as they walk into your classroom will mean that pupils *want* to arrive early and start working immediately. This makes a very good impression on any observer or inspector that may one day visit your lesson. It also avoids the time wasted for your lesson to commence, particularly if the class have just had PE!

An alternative to these little, open-ended challenges is an ongoing task which students can revisit at the beginning of every lesson (and in their own time, too, if they wish). For example:

- Make as many positive integers as you can, using exactly 4 fours (and any mathematical operations).[7]
- How many squares are there on a chessboard?[8]
- How many ways are there to make 123456789 = 100 true by inserting addition and/or subtraction signs between the digits on the left-hand side only?[9]

Once all the pupils have arrived for your lesson, an effective starter is needed to help them focus on learning, make them think and provide a sense of curiosity to maintain interest. The following tried and tested activities are particularly useful when it comes to engaging learners in maths lessons.

7 For example: 1 = (4 + 4) / (4 + 4); 2 = (4 / 4) + (4 / 4); 3 = (4 + 4 + 4) / 4, etc.

8 There are 204.

9 There are 11. For example: 1 + 23 - 4 + 56 + 7 + 8 + 9 = 100.

## If this is the answer, what is the question?[10]

The teacher provides the answer and students think of as many questions as possible. For example, if the answer is 5 metres, what is the question? Half of 10 metres? Double 250 centimetres? A tenth of 50 metres? The approximate height of a tree? The length of a square with area 25 metres squared? The length 4.78 metres correct to one significant figure? The possibilities are endless! The aim of this activity is to reward good thinking as opposed to simply listing the most questions.

## Centre of the universe[11]

Clear the decks! Create some space in the classroom and ask students to agree or disagree with the statements you provide. The closer to the centre of the room they stand, the more they agree. The further away from the centre of the room, the more they disagree. Students must justify their position and, after listening to their peers, everybody is given a chance to change their mind. For example, as an opening gambit to a lesson on probability, ask students how far they agree with the statement, 'The probability of it raining tomorrow is 50% because it will either be raining or it will not be raining.'

10 This idea has been adapted from Keeling (2009: 12).
11 This idea has been adapted from Ginnis (2002: 83).

## Diamond ranking

Arrange nine expressions or calculations written on cards into the diamond shape below:

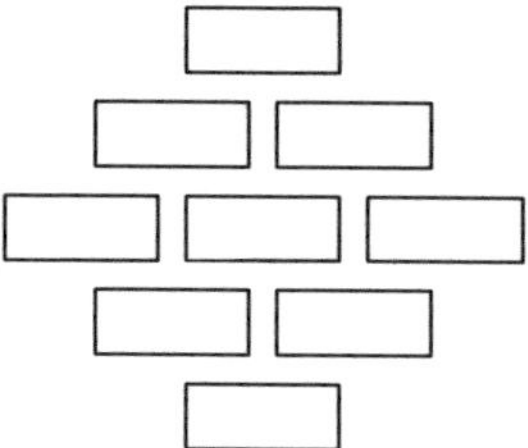

The card at the top must have the greatest value, followed by two cards of less value (but equal to one another), followed by a row of three, then two, and finally the card with the least value at the bottom.

For example, if $n = 4$, students must place these expressions into the diamond:

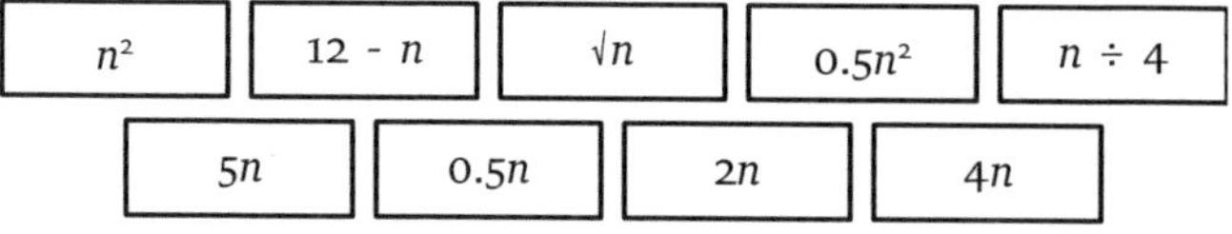


Or, for younger children:

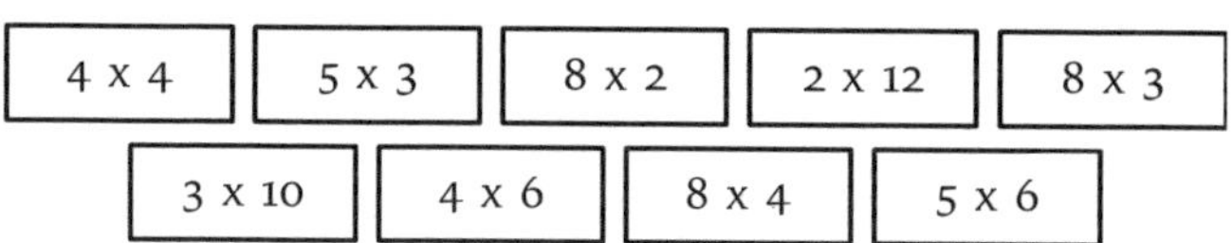

## Deliberately wrong answers

Get out the red pens! The teacher provides deliberately wrong answers to maths problems. Students, in the role of teacher, need to mark the work, correcting errors as they arise. To make things a little harder, throw in one or two correct answers as well. Finish by asking students to write some advice to the author of the deliberately wrong answers about how to improve their work.

## Mystery bag

Put an object with a connection to the lesson into a bag or box. Students place their hand into the bag or box and attempt to guess what the object is. Alternatively, students can ask 20 questions or describe the object to teammates to guess. For example, to capture the imagination of the class for a lesson on sequences, place a sunflower into the mystery bag as an introduction to Fibonacci.[12]

## Taboo

Students attempt to describe a focus word without reading aloud any of the 'taboo' words given. For example, a pupil might be asked to describe 'radius' without using the words 'circle', 'straight', 'centre', 'circumference' or 'sphere'. As a

12 The Fibonacci numbers appear in many places in nature. On the head of a sunflower, for example, seeds are arranged in spirals, one set turning clockwise and another anticlockwise. If you count the number of spirals in either direction you will, almost always, find a Fibonacci number. The same is true for pine cones, broccoli florets, cauliflowers and pineapples!

follow-on, pupils can write a formal definition for the focus word using all of the taboo words listed (e.g. 'A radius is a straight line from the centre to the circumference of a circle or sphere').

## Pelmanism

This simple game is more commonly known as 'concentration' or 'pairs'. A student turns face up two cards of their choice. If they match, the student takes the cards and has another go. If they do not match, they are turned face down again and it is the next student's turn. Depending on the theme of the lesson, examples of matching pairs might include:

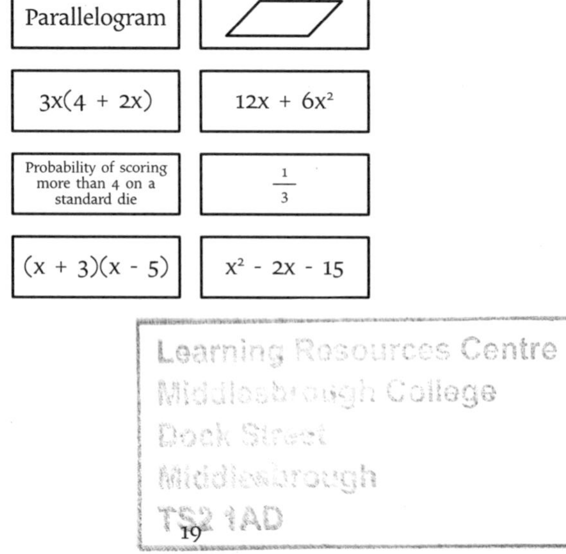

## Checklist: engaging learners in maths lessons

- Ensure the pace is 'just right' – fast enough to maintain interest and slow enough to enable deep learning. ☑
- Make use of the time when students are arriving with an open-ended challenge. ☑
- Hook learners into learning with a short, snappy starter activity. ☑
- Use movement to bring about a change in pace. ☑
- Minimise teacher-talk. ☑
- Link learning to students' lives and real-world problem solving. ☑
- Introduce friendly controversy. ☑

# Chapter 2
# Challenging Learners in Maths Lessons

Given the right set of circumstances, all students can make progress – particularly when the teacher is determined that they will. In the perfect maths lesson, teachers help students to appreciate that effort is required for success by ensuring that the work is perplexing, mystifying and delightfully baffling.

> In solving problems, teachers aim to foster the attitude that students, even the most able, should expect to struggle and, indeed, welcome the challenge.
>
> Ofsted (2012b: 2)

Ideally, you should be aiming just beyond the point students have already reached – occupying a space right at the edge of their ability. Lessons should require learners to apply their mathematical knowledge, skills and experience to new and unknown situations which, when mastered, will promote a sense of achievement. In seeking solutions which are not obvious students are able to develop resilience and confidence. Remember, 'spoon feeding in the long run teaches us nothing but the shape of the spoon'.[1]

> Teaching engages and includes all pupils, with work that is challenging enough and that meets their individual needs, including for the most able pupils.
>
> Ofsted (2014: 37)

Introducing challenge into maths lessons does not require significant amounts of preparation on the part of the teacher. Challenge can be woven into learning by asking the right questions in the right way. Effective questioning is a central tenet of the perfect maths lesson because deep learning begins with questions, not answers. Although teachers cannot successfully plan every question, they can plan a few questions successfully.

At the planning stage it is useful to ask:

- Will my questions focus thinking on the key concepts?
- Will my questions help me to gauge where learners are in their learning?
- Are too many of my questions closed?

1 Attributed to E. M. Forster, *The Observer* (7 October, 1951).

- Will my questions promote the accurate use of mathematical vocabulary?
- What is this question trying to achieve?
- Have I allowed time to review these questions at the end of the lesson?

Maths teachers need to differentiate their questions to ensure that learners are appropriately challenged and can make progress. 'Rich' questions encourage learners to make links with previous learning, stimulate thinking, reveal misconceptions and generate even more questions.

> Effective teachers anticipate pupils' likely misconceptions and are skilled in choosing resources and particular examples to expose misconceptions and check that their understanding is secure.
>
> Ofsted (2008a: 39)

Think about the difference between the following questions:

*Is 2 a prime number?*

*Why is it true that 2 is the only even prime number?*

The first question is closed, requires little thinking by the student and does not help the teacher to assess their understanding (with a 50% chance of success, the answer is little more than a good guess!). The second question is more open, requires the student to apply their knowledge and helps the teacher make a judgement about the quality of the learning.

Consider these further examples of rich questions:

*What is the area of a square with the length 8cm?*

I suggest becomes:

*Put these three squares in size order, from smallest to largest. Square A has a perimeter of 64cm. Square B has a length of 64cm. Square C has an area of 64cm$^2$.*

*What is a rhombus?*

I suggest becomes:

*In what ways is a rhombus like a rectangle? In what ways is it different?*

In these examples, the teacher is encouraging thinking at a higher level so that students are not only required to define and recall but also to compare, contrast and relate. Such degrees of difficulty are classified as being in the cognitive domain of Bloom's taxonomy, namely:

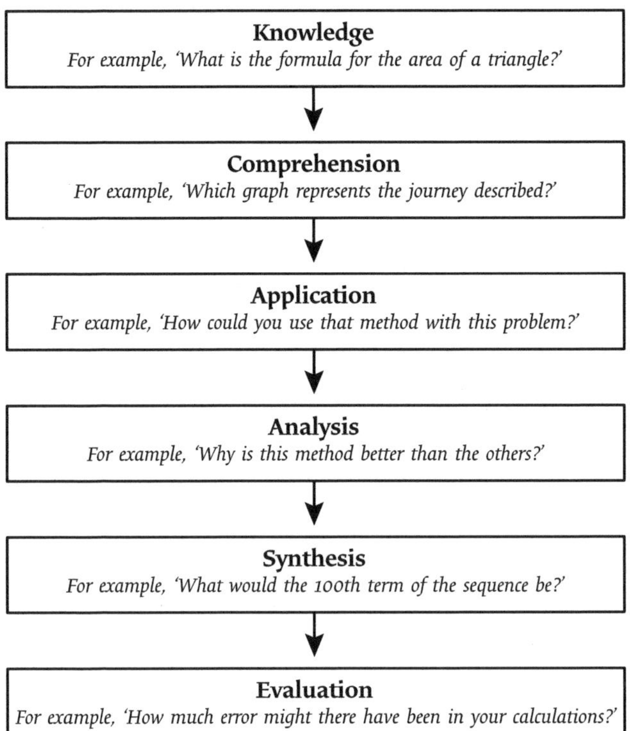


Maths teachers ask a lot of questions, many of them associated with the 'knowledge' and 'comprehension' categories. These types of questions are not bad, per se, but using them all the time is! Questions which promote sophisticated thinking need to be peppered throughout the perfect maths lesson, affording more able learners, in particular, the opportunity to demonstrate the skills associated with higher national curriculum levels.

| **Type of thinking** | **Mathematical skills demonstrated** | **Questioning words** |
|---|---|---|
| Knowledge | For example:<br>Recall of number facts<br>Knowledge of shape properties | List, define, collect, identify, label, show, name, state, etc. |
| Comprehension | For example:<br>Interpreting graphs<br>Describing trends | Interpret, estimate, describe, express, continue, etc. |
| Application | For example:<br>Solve equations<br>Calculate areas | Apply, demonstrate, calculate, solve, change, construct, etc. |
| Analysis | For example:<br>Classify shapes<br>Ordering | Analyse, order, explain, select, compare, classify, arrange, etc. |

| **Type of thinking** | **Mathematical skills demonstrated** | **Questioning words** |
|---|---|---|
| Synthesis | For example:<br>Make predictions<br>Generalise from given facts | Combine, rearrange, substitute, design, formulate, generalise, etc. |
| Evaluation | For example:<br>Recognise bias<br>Compare methods | Assess, decide, rank, select, conclude, test, etc. |

> In a few good and outstanding lessons, pupils were given substantial problems to solve that required them to think hard about the problem, draw on their previous knowledge, and grapple with applying it in a new, unusual or complex context.
>
> Ofsted (2012a: 31)

The example below is an activity based on the properties of numbers which challenges learners and demands higher order thinking (it's also really good fun and fosters competition with oneself).

*Write the numbers 1 to 16 (one in each box) so that they satisfy the conditions in both the row and column.*

| | Prime number | Odd number | Factor of 16 | Even number |
|---|---|---|---|---|
| Number less than 7 | | | | |
| Factor of 36 | | | | |
| Number less than 12 | | | | |
| Numbers between 11 and 17 | | | | |

In the next example, pairs of students are required to pick two cells by rolling dice, multiply them by expanding brackets and simplify the result.[2] The level of challenge is then increased by asking pairs to swap their simplified solutions with another pair and, by factorisation, identify which two cells had originally led to each of the answers.

2 Inspired by an idea attributed to Rebecca Richardson in Griffith and Burns (2012: 31).

| | | | | | | |
|---|---|---|---|---|---|---|
| **6** | $2x$ | $(x + 1)$ | $(x + 6)$ | 10 | $6x$ | $(x + 30)$ |
| **5** | $(x + 50)$ | 8 | $(x - 10)$ | $x^4$ | $(x - 50)$ | $x^3$ |
| **4** | $(x + 8)$ | $4x$ | $-2x$ | $(x - 15)$ | $(x - 4)$ | $3x$ |
| **3** | $(x + 4)$ | 6 | $(x + 25)$ | $(x - 8)$ | $(x - 1)$ | $-x$ |
| **2** | $x$ | $(x + 5)$ | $(x - 2)$ | 25 | $(x - 7)$ | $(x - 30)$ |
| **1** | $(x + 20)$ | $(x - 5)$ | $10x$ | $2x^2$ | 5 | $2x^5$ |
| | ***1*** | ***2*** | ***3*** | ***4*** | ***5*** | ***6*** |

Introducing challenge to maths lessons depends not only on what you ask but also on how you ask it. If questions are too easy or too difficult, or if they are targeted inappropriately, then they are unlikely to be successful. Questions must provide opportunities for learners to see how others are thinking and students must always feel safe to respond. The following useful techniques are tried and tested in the classroom:

- Provide thinking time – no less than five seconds per question. Do not be afraid of the silence!
- Follow-up answers – 'Tell me more.' 'Do you agree?' 'Can you elaborate?'
- No hands up – keep students on their toes and expect everybody to be involved in the learning.
- Ask for summaries – 'Can you summarise your partner's point?'
- Pose, pause, pounce, bounce – ask a question, provide thinking time, choose a student to share their answer and then pass the answer to another student to respond to (see Harrison and Howard, 2009: 15).
- Explain the thinking – 'Can you explain how you got to that answer?'
- Use mini-whiteboards – assess understanding by asking everybody to reveal their answer.
- Phone a friend – 'Why don't you call on somebody else in the class to respond?'

Challenge in the perfect maths lesson must also be matched to students' learning needs by means of careful differentiation. 'Differentiation by outcome' is no longer considered good practice and too often results in some children coasting and others getting little further in the lesson than writing the title and date in their books. Instead, maths teachers must ensure that differentiation is purposeful, allowing learners to make maximum progress and giving them an equal opportunity to experience success.

> When judging achievement, inspectors must have regard for pupils' starting points in terms of their prior attainment and age. This includes the progress that the lowest attaining pupils are making and its effect on raising their attainment, and the progress that the most able are making towards attaining the highest levels and grades.
>
> Ofsted (2014: 31)

You can enable the lowest attaining students to access learning by:

- Providing key words and word banks for written response questions.
- Providing visual aids, charts or graphic organisers.
- Sensitively designing different tasks for different pupils (with the same learning objective).

- Spending more time with small groups.
- Increasing the amount of time spent modelling the learning.
- Allowing students to preview any text which will be used in the next lesson.
- Introducing intermediary learning objectives to scaffold the learning for some children.
- Making good use of learning support assistants, trainee teachers, older students or peers.

The example below shows the previously seen activity based on the properties of numbers after having been sensitively redesigned for less able students without changing the learning objective.

*Write the numbers 1 to 9 (one in each box) so that they satisfy the conditions in both the row and column.*

| | Number between 5 and 9 | Square number | Prime number |
|---|---|---|---|
| Factor of 6 | | | |
| Even number | | | |
| Odd number | | | |

Here is a second example, this time based on the expansion and factorisation task.

| **6** | 2 | $(x + 1)$ | $(2x + 6)$ | 10 | 6 | $(x + 2)$ |
|---|---|---|---|---|---|---|
| **5** | $(x - 6)$ | 8 | $(x - 10)$ | 100 | $(x - 3)$ | 3 |
| **4** | $(x + 8)$ | 4 | 30 | $(x + 7)$ | $(5x - 4)$ | 15 |
| **3** | $(2x + 4)$ | 5 | $(x + 3)$ | $(x - 8)$ | $(x - 1)$ | 1 |
| **2** | 11 | $(x + 5)$ | $(3x - 2)$ | 25 | $(2x - 7)$ | $(x + 10)$ |
| **1** | $(x + 20)$ | $(4x - 5)$ | 12 | 9 | 7 | 20 |
| | **1** | **2** | **3** | **4** | **5** | **6** |

In the perfect maths lesson, however, teachers must also find a way to help all children *think mathematically* to enable them to access learning. The practical and theoretical aspects of mathematics have earned it a special place as a core subject in our schools, yet too often a focus is given to memorising instead of understanding maths. For many children, procedural knowledge and rote learning have led to a void in understanding which prevents them from making the expected progress. They require *conceptual understanding* in order to comprehend mathematical operations and relations before they are able to apply mathematical ideas to new situations. By assisting students to understand the concept underpinning a process, they are more likely to correctly apply that process in an unfamiliar context.

> Frequently, [pupils'] comments showed appreciation of their teachers' efforts to support them as they approached examinations, but also exposed recognition that their understanding of mathematics was insecure. An able pupil summed this up: 'You need to understand and not just do it. You think you know how to do it but you get to an exam and you can't. You realise that nobody's told you why it works and why you do what you do, so you can't remember it.'
>
> Ofsted (2012a: 19)

Continuing the theme of the properties of numbers, consider how this introduction to prime numbers supports mathematical thinking:

*Draw as many rectangles as you can with an area of 12cm*$^2$.

The possible solutions are:

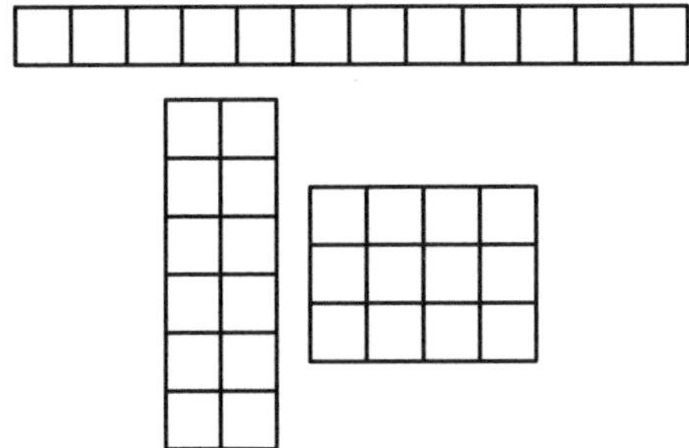

This gives us the factors of 12 (1, 2, 3, 4, 6 and 12).

*Now draw as many rectangles as you can with an area of 11cm*$^2$.

The possible solutions are:

This gives us the factors of 11 (1 and 11).

By repeating the exercise for other numbers, students will begin to see that certain examples share the property of only having one possible rectangle. These numbers are the primes which we can now see have two distinct factors, themselves and 1. Students may also notice something interesting about the square numbers too!

Cuisenaire rods are another useful tool for promoting mathematical thinking in the classroom.[3] They allow students to explore the properties of numbers physically and visually as they handle and manipulate the rods. The ten coloured rods vary in integer lengths from 1–10cm and can enrich the conceptual understanding of arithmetic, fractions and more.

Consider what students might learn from the following arrangement of Cuisenaire rods:

<table>
<tr><td colspan="10">Orange</td></tr>
<tr><td colspan="5">Yellow</td><td colspan="5">Yellow</td></tr>
<tr><td colspan="2">Red</td><td colspan="2">Red</td><td colspan="2">Red</td><td colspan="2">Red</td><td colspan="2">Red</td></tr>
<tr><td></td><td></td><td></td><td></td><td></td><td></td><td></td><td></td><td></td><td></td></tr>
</table>

Yellow + Yellow = Orange

Orange – Yellow = Yellow

Half of Orange is Yellow

One-fifth of Orange is Red

One-half of Orange = Five-tenths of Orange

The factors of 10 are 1, 2, 5 and 10

3 See www.cuisenaire.co.uk for more information or to purchase your own set of rods.

2 / 5 = 4 / 10

1 / 5 = 0.2 = 20%

10 is not a prime number

There are many ways to teach long multiplication, each with their merits and pitfalls. However, the following approach can be very useful in the development of conceptual understanding. Consider the calculation 38 × 42:

| | **30** | **8** |
|---|---|---|
| **40** | 1200 | 320 |
| **2** | 60 | 16 |

Leading to 38 × 42 = 1200 + 320 + 60 + 16 = 1596. This can now be applied to algebraic calculations, often with little or no input from the teacher. For example, consider the expansion of $(n + 8)(n + 2)$:

| | $\boldsymbol{n}$ | **8** |
|---|---|---|
| $\boldsymbol{n}$ | $n^2$ | $8n$ |
| **2** | $2n$ | 16 |

Leading to $(n + 8)(n + 2) = n^2 + 8n + 2n + 16 = n^2 + 10n + 16$. This approach also enables the learner to tackle other numerical calculations (such as those involving three or more digits) and algebraic calculations (such as those involving three of more terms) without difficulty.[4]

> In the very best schools ... [teaching] challenged [learners] to think for themselves, for instance by suggesting how to tackle a new problem or comparing alternative approaches. Teachers' explanations were kept suitably brief and focused on the underlying concepts, how the work linked with previous learning and other topics and, where appropriate, an efficient standard method.
>
> Ofsted (2012a: 23)

## Checklist: challenging learners in maths lessons

- If it makes your brain go 'ouch' it means you're learning!
- Introduce challenge by asking the right questions in the right way.
- Ensure questions are 'rich' and promote higher order thinking. 

4 Popular approaches such as FOIL (First, Outside, Inside, Last) cannot be applied to calculations of the form $(x + y)(a + b + c)$, for example, and should be avoided.

- Let them think! Provide wait time after every question. ☑
- No hands up (unless they are asking you a question). ☑
- Pose, pause, pounce, bounce – when asking questions in the classroom think 'basketball' as opposed to 'table tennis'. ☑
- Conceptual understanding must underpin procedural knowledge. ☑
- Add extra challenge and embed skills by letting students teach new examples to each other or to younger students (see Chapter 3). ☑

# Chapter 3
# Independent Learning in Maths Lessons

In the perfect maths lesson, pupils are motivated to take responsibility for their learning and work with their teacher to structure the learning environment. Promoting independence unshackles the learner from prescriptive, narrow and specific learning experiences by providing a degree of autonomy over what and how they will learn.

Independent learning in maths lessons is about:

- Understanding the aims of the learning.
- Children organising themselves and their learning.
- Solving complex problems.
- Learners finding, collecting and using information.
- Making choices as individuals and as a group.
- Students making decisions about how to move forward in their learning.
- Accountability (yours and theirs).
- Whetting children's appetite to learn.

Independent learning in maths lessons is *not* about:

- Removing the need for 'traditional' instruction.
- Preventing teachers from modelling learning.
- Making children work in isolation.
- Minimising opportunities for collaboration and cooperation.
- Dumbing down.
- Avoiding new knowledge and understanding.

> Critically, pupils were directly engaged in mathematics for a substantial portion of each lesson. As a result, they had time to develop a high degree of competence and to tackle challenging, varied questions and problems that helped to deepen their understanding. Pupils worked on a mix of group tasks, exploratory activities in which they tried to devise their own methods, and exercises completed individually. The exercises allowed pupils to progress from routine practice of skills to two-step questions, where the method was not immediately apparent, and questions with unusual twists that required some adaptation to the standard method.
>
> Ofsted (2012a: 23)

Independence, then, is what really connects the *teaching* with the *learning*. Direct instruction on the part of the teacher (that is, deciding the learning objectives, modelling the learning, monitoring and evaluating understanding and tying the learning together – see Hattie, 2009: 206) is essential if students are to make progress. However, students learn even better when they can self-select or self-generate learning tasks, collaborate with peers and self-regulate their own learning (Nuthall, 2007: 156). In the perfect maths lesson, therefore, the act of teaching is something done *with* students and not *to* them.

Of course, independence in maths lessons does not just happen; it must be taught. This means that learners need to be given more responsibility for their own learning and teachers must provide opportunities for students to self-manage their learning. Often this involves students doing different things from one another in the classroom. Individuals or small groups may need to approach mathematical problems in different ways; some by discussion, some by quiet contemplation, others by experimentation. Independence also involves giving students a choice (or, perhaps, a *sense* of choice) and ownership over their learning so that they are more motivated to achieve success and their confidence to embark on future, challenging learning is heightened.

At the planning stage it is useful to think about:

- Are the learning objectives clear? Will students know what they are expected to achieve? Have success criteria been shared?
- Is my lesson plan flexible enough for students to determine the direction their learning takes?

- Are opportunities for reflection built into the lesson?
- What choices will students be able to make about their learning?
- How will learners be held accountable for their own learning?
- Who is doing all the work in this lesson? Me or them?

Organising pupils into groups, and assigning roles to each member of the group, can be an effective way to promote independent learning in maths lessons. Roles might include a facilitator, a time keeper, an envoy, a researcher, a note taker or a learning spy (who feeds back to the class about the learning in the group).[1] This approach ensures that students understand what they are trying to learn by keeping them focused on the objectives of the task and helps them to be accountable for the part they have to play in the learning.

It is also necessary to organise the classroom to maximise opportunities for independent learning. Do you use *teaching* resources (locked away in a filing cabinet until you determine they are required) or *learning* resources (readily available for students to call on if they require support)? Providing access to centimetre squared paper, 100 squares, number lines, graph paper, protractors, calculators, isometric paper, multilink cubes, Cuisenaire rods, coins, playing cards and fraction walls gives students a choice about how they tackle problems in maths and allows them to explore new ideas.

---

1 Learning spies are explained in detail in Didau (2012: 93).

Too many young people believe that, in the maths classroom, getting things 'right' or 'wrong' equates to 'success' or 'failure'. However, making mistakes acts as a gateway to new learning because success is generally predicated on a series of failures. Carol Dweck warns us of the dangers of praising 'perfection' in the maths classroom:

> When we say to children, 'Wow, you did that so quickly!' or 'Look, you didn't make any mistakes!' what message are we sending? We are telling them that what we prize are speed and perfection. Speed and perfection are the enemy of difficult learning.
>
> Dweck (2006: 178)

Dweck explains that if teachers link being 'smart' with being fast and perfect, children will avoid taking on anything challenging. If your students are completing the mathematics you give them quickly and perfectly, then praise should be denied. Instead, when this happens, she suggests that the teacher says, 'Whoops, I guess that was too easy. I apologise for wasting your time. Let's do something you can really learn from!'

Such is the fear of failure in maths lessons that pupils often choose to opt out of challenging learning and the words 'I'm stuck' resonate throughout the classroom. In the perfect maths lesson, getting stuck is celebrated because it triggers new learning and helps children to get better at maths. Some powerful responses to 'I'm stuck' for teachers include:

*'If I offered you £1 million to get unstuck, what would you do differently?'*

*'You're stuck? Great! That means you are about to learn something new!'*

*'Imagine you weren't stuck – what would you do then?'*

*'What are the people who are not stuck doing differently?'*

*'You can't do it ... yet.'*

And what about these alternatives to 'I'm stuck' for students? Try displaying them on a poster in your classroom:

*'May I have some more information please?'*

*'Would you please repeat the question?'*

*'May I have some more time to think?'*

*'Where can I find more information about that?'*

*'May I ask a friend for help?'*

Understanding learning as a journey that starts with not knowing and ends in knowing 'how to do it' has been outlined in Beere (2012a: 72) and adapted by many teachers since. The use of a learning continuum based on the objectives for the lesson reinforces to learners that getting stuck is not synonymous with failure. Instead, getting stuck, making mistakes and finding things a bit tricky become part of the learning journey in which many steps are taken towards a learning goal. This demonstrates that, whatever level you may be working at, you are making progress. Learning continuums also allow maths teachers to assess progress during the lesson and are explored in more depth in Chapter 4.

Helping learners to get themselves unstuck without relying on the teacher is an important precept for developing independence in maths lessons. Teachers need to rein in their impulse to answer students' questions, instead responding by asking the question back. For example, if a pupil asks, 'Why is the answer negative?', the teacher replies, 'Good question. Why do you think the answer is negative?' The use of a 'stuck cycle', displayed prominently in the classroom, also encourages independent learning by helping students to seek appropriate support when needed.

The steps of the stuck cycle might look something like this:

Step 1: Pause and think about the question again.

Step 2: Try breaking the problem down into smaller steps.

Step 3: Look at the board or your book for clues.

Step 4: Think about how you solved previous problems.

Step 5: Ask your learning partner.

Step 6: Ask the teacher.

For younger children, it can be useful to simplify the stuck cycle using the 3B4Me technique (Brain, Book, Buddy, Boss).[2] This works by coaching children to do the following if they hit a brick wall in their learning: first, stop, relax and

2 For a full explanation see Smith (2010: 55).

think about the problem again. Next, look back through your book (or on the board) for similar examples that could help you here. Then, discuss the problem with a partner and, if they can do it, ask them to explain *how* they did it to you (not simply copy the answer). Finally, pop up your hand and ask the teacher for guidance. Both of these strategies provide pupils with opportunities to self-regulate, and be responsible for, their learning.

> Sometimes, a pupil is heard to say to the teacher, 'When I am stuck and ask you a question, you don't tell me the answer. You just ask me another question!' This is often a sign of a skilful teacher, whose questions are helping to get to the bottom of what the pupil is thinking and hence what the difficulty is. Carefully constructed questions can enable the pupil to resolve the difficulty themselves.
>
> Ofsted (2008a: 48)

Setting great homework is one of the best ways to get children learning independently. Homework is no longer considered to be something which must be completed at home. Many teachers run clubs before or after the school day and children often choose to collaborate during lunch breaks, in the library or online. Just like the perfect maths lesson, maths homework needs to engage and challenge learners. Poorly designed homework is unlikely to capture the imagination of your class and often leads to an increased workload for the teacher. Conversely, carefully constructed homework tasks shift the balance of leading learning in the direction of the student, making them accountable for taking decisions to move their learning forward.

One way to get your students engaged with their homework is to use a 'takeaway homework' menu.[3] The idea is simple: set your students free to try out different ideas by providing opportunities for creativity and choice. Far from replacing more traditional models of maths homework (which largely focus on consolidating skills through repetition), this approach complements the superb work already taking place in your classroom and can be woven throughout a topic or unit. Set students a target, for example to gain a total of six 'chillies' over the course of the topic, and leave the rest to them!

**Mild**

Create a factsheet about this topic. Include at least three worked examples.

Create a set of flashcards about this topic. Include both questions and answers plus key words and definitions.

Create a worksheet about this topic. Design the questions carefully and produce an answer guide on a separate sheet. For an extra chilli, give your worksheet to another student and mark their work.

3 This idea has been adapted from McGill (2013: 71).

**Medium**

Create a 'maths mat' about this topic. Include key words, at least three worked examples and some images or diagrams.

Design a webpage about this topic. Include an introduction, worked examples, key words, images or diagrams and links to other helpful websites.

Write a memorable poem or song about this topic. Include key vocabulary. For an extra chilli, perform your poem or song to the class.

**Hot**

Plan a starter activity on this topic (a carefully designed quiz or recap activity). For an extra chilli, teach the class using your activity.

Create a short film about this topic. Include a full explanation of the topic, worked examples, useful tips and hints and a summary of the key points. For an extra chilli, share your video with the class.

Make a board or card game about this topic. Think carefully about how players will score points and how the game will allow them to practise their maths skills. For an extra chilli, play your game with other students in your class.

This approach to homework fosters independence in learners and also helps them to become more resilient and resourceful as they grapple with the demands of these creative challenges. Takeaway homework activities are easily adapted to suit pairs or small groups and, importantly, afford students the opportunity to teach others. In the example above, incentives are given to encourage students to share their work. As a result, they are required to think more carefully about the topic so that they can explain it to their peers or younger students and, in so doing, deepen their understanding of the mathematical concept (see Chapter 4 for ideas about marking, feedback and Dedicated Improvement and Reflection Time (DIRT)).

During your lesson, the following tried and tested activities are very effective when it comes to developing independent learning in maths lessons.

## Question generator

Ask students to generate as many questions as they can think of on the given topic, first by thinking on their own and then by refining questions in pairs or small groups. By using sticky notes, each group can stick their questions to the board (or a dedicated 'wonder wall') ranking them in order of interest. The remainder of the lesson (or series of lessons) is built around these questions.

## Circus time[4]

Set out the classroom so that desks form a series of 'learning stations'. Design a number of tasks relating to the learning objectives with clear instruction sheets at each of the stations. Students are permitted to roam around the classroom (or, if preferred, form a carousel) visiting each station and undertaking the task outlined. Short tasks might be concluded within one lesson or longer tasks might be completed over a series of lessons. This works particularly well with, for example, probability experiments.

## Conversion

Students are provided with material presented in one format and asked to convert it to another. They might turn the words from a page in a textbook into a concept map, a flowchart, a Venn diagram, a graph or an ordered list. For example, students might convert images of triangles into the following flowchart:

4 This idea has been adapted from Ginnis (2002: 85).

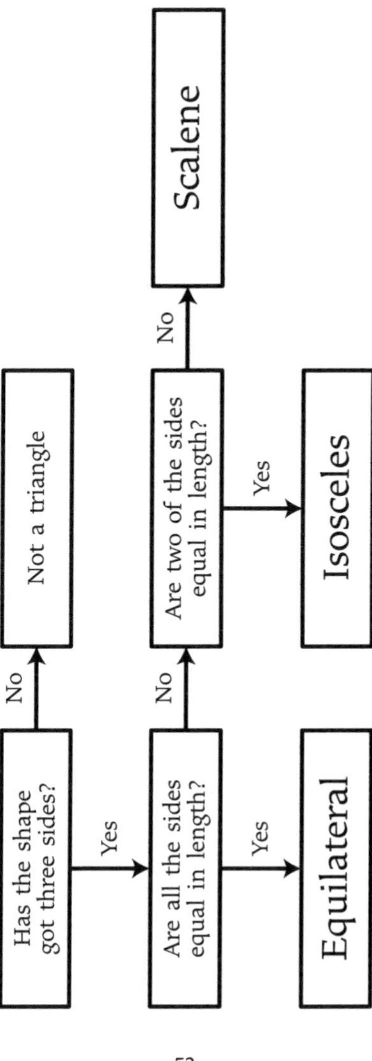
Has the shape got three sides?
No
Not a triangle
Yes
Are all the sides equal in length?
Yes
Equilateral
No
Are two of the sides equal in length?
Yes
Isosceles
No
Scalene

## Speed dating[5]

Students sit in pairs, facing one another. They are each provided with a question on a card linked to the learning objectives which are discussed, in turn, for a fixed (and normally brief) period of time. Partners are then swapped and the process repeated. For example, one partner may have a card with an expression which must be factorised, the other an expression which must be expanded. If anybody becomes stuck, their partner demonstrates how to solve the problem.

## Twenty questions

In groups, students are given a set of cards depicting numbers, shapes, key words, formulae, sequences or operations which need to be learned. In turns, students select a card and the group must identify the number/shape/word/formula/sequence/operation by asking up to 20 questions to which the card holder can only answer 'yes' or 'no'.

## Who am I?

This is a variant of 'twenty questions'. In groups, students are given a set of cards describing numbers, shapes, key words, formulae, sequences or operations which need to be learned. In turns, students select a card and read the clues aloud one by one until somebody in the group correctly guesses the answer. If nobody in the group guesses correctly, the reader

5 This idea has been adapted from Hodgson (2009: 46–47).

wins the card. For example, 'Who am I? I am a two-dimensional shape. I am a polygon. I am irregular. I have three sides. None of my sides are equal in length. None of my angles are equal either!' (I am a scalene triangle.)

## One-to-one

Divide the topic being learned into two halves. Give the first sub-topic to one half of the class and the second sub-topic to the other. Students must master the materials they have been given producing a poster/crib sheet/revision aid before they are required to teach the topic to a student from the other half of the class.

## Pub quiz

This is a great way to give a class test without it feeling quite so dull and burdensome. The 'pub' quiz can be split into rounds and, for authenticity, drinks, nibbles and music can be provided! For example, rounds might test multiplication tables, mathematical vocabulary, circle theorems, names of 3D shapes or mental methods for calculating percentages. Better still, small groups can each be responsible for writing the questions and answers for a round.

## Back-to-back

As the name suggests, students sit back-to-back. One student is given a diagram which they must describe, in exact detail, to their partner. The second student must recreate the diagram with the aim of producing a precise replica. This works particularly with, for example, constructions and bearings.

## Checklist: independent learning in maths lessons

- Provide a sense of choice about what or how students will learn. ☑
- Help them see mistakes as an opportunity to learn. ☑
- Organise learners into groups and assign roles to individuals. ☑
- Make learning resources available. Always. ☑
- Help them get unstuck by referring to the success criteria at the end of their mathematical 'journey' in the lesson (also see Chapter 4). ☑
- Rein in your impulse to answer questions – get them to think through the answers themselves. ☑
- Set great homework that makes a difference to their learning. ☑

## Chapter 4

# Assessment of, for and as Learning in Maths Lessons

Effective assessment is the key lever for personalising learning in the perfect maths lesson. Assessment can be done to, with or by students but, in its most emancipating form, assessment always results in the learner moving forward in their learning. Good assessment, in whichever guise, is accurate, focused, reliable, fair and useful.

At the planning stage it is useful to think about:

- Why am I assessing?
- What am I assessing?
- What assessment method should I use?
- How will I use the information from this assessment?

Likewise, prior to (or during) the learning students should be encouraged to think about:

- What do I already know about this topic?

- What methods have I already learned that could help me here?
- What would the success criteria look like?
- Have I done anything like this before? Could that help me now?
- Do I understand this concept?

There are distinct differences between assessment *of*, *for* and *as* learning and each has a part to play in maths lessons.

Assessment *of* learning is usually summative and takes place periodically, often at the end of a topic or series of lessons. It is designed to provide a judgement about what a student understands, commonly for a wide audience including parents and other teachers. It is important that judgments are fair and based on a variety of contexts.

Assessment *for* learning is usually formative and takes place during (and often between) lessons. It is designed to help learners improve by understanding the aim of their learning, where they are in relation to this aim and how they can close the gap between the two. It is important that feedback is descriptive and immediate, providing direction to the learner.

Assessment *as* learning is formative and permeates the learning in every lesson. It is designed to help learners improve by developing the capacity to assess their own understanding with increasing independence and metacognitive awareness. It is important that opportunities for students to practise self-monitoring and evaluation are woven into lessons (see the learning continuum later in this chapter).

In the perfect maths lesson, teachers should:

- Share clear learning objectives at the start of every lesson.
- Provide regular opportunities for students to mark their own work and that of others.
- Focus on the process or method employed, not just the final answer.
- Provide regular opportunities for students to read the work of others and comment on the mathematics used.
- Encourage students to devise their own questions (and, perhaps, their own maths tests).
- Explain levels and grades in simple language so that students can use them against agreed criteria.
- Help students to understand the purpose of the work and the success criteria.
- Comment explicitly on the mathematical aspects of the work.
- Ensure feedback is a two-way process between teacher and learner.

> [The most skilful] teachers were usually also skilled in drawing learning together at key moments of the lesson and, rather than just recapping on the lesson to that point, they encouraged pupils to show what they had learnt. They gave them opportunities to discuss their learning and develop their understanding. For example, these teachers used 'talk partners' to explore an open-ended question or gave groups different questions to answer. These approaches encouraged pupils to give feedback and explain their ideas to others.
>
> Ofsted (2008b: 13)

Providing feedback to learners should always take the form of identifying areas of strength and giving focused, clear and constructive advice about how to improve. The most regular (and most powerful) form of feedback is oral feedback. It is important that oral feedback is positive and sensitive so that it does not undermine the confidence of learners. It is useful to give 'a medal and a mission' by celebrating what has been done well and identifying the next steps.[1] This ensures your comments remain focused on helping the learner to make progress. However, be mindful not to overload students with verbal feedback. You need to limit comments to one or two things that the learner can change. It is also beneficial to invite children to comment on the things that you do as well. They are well able to appraise the pace of the lesson, the

1 For more on this strategy see Black and Wiliam (1998).

degree of challenge you have presented and tell you about the extent to which you have sparked their imagination!

Good oral feedback allows maths teachers to:

- Praise
- Challenge
- Correct
- Clarify
- Confirm
- Redirect
- Refocus

> [In the most effective lessons] teachers listened to pupils carefully and observed their work throughout the lesson. They aimed to identify any potential misconceptions or barriers to understanding key concepts, and responded accordingly.
>
> Ofsted (2008a: 13)

Written feedback, done well, is worthwhile but it should not be unduly burdensome on the teacher. It is important that written feedback does not immediately focus on errors but begins with praise. Likewise, where errors have been repeated it can be counterproductive to correct every mistake (a lot of red ink can be a real blow to confidence). Instead, students should be encouraged to revisit their work, making corrections for themselves. Try saving time by, instead of correcting calculations on behalf of the student, simply identifying how many errors have been made. A student whose work is returned with the number '3' written on it by the teacher must now check each of their answers to identify which three are incorrect. Once identified (by reviewing success criteria and collaborating with their peers), the student can go about correcting their errors.

When providing written comments, teachers must always be specific, indicating what the learner needs to do to improve their mathematics. Your advice should prompt reflection and require action on the part of the learner. Therefore, it is essential that students are given time in lessons to read and respond to your comments. There is little value in 'ticking and flicking' – one-step problems can be marked in class by the learners. Reserve your time and energy for providing expert advice specific to each child.

Good written feedback should have the following features:

- Linked to the learning objectives.
- Confirms what has been done well.
- Gives clear direction for how to improve.
- Motivates students to correct errors.
- Does not compare one learner with another.
- Provides an opportunity for students to respond.

> Very effective assessment for learning was usually supported by detailed and constructive marking of written work. In the best examples, pupils were made aware of what they had achieved, what they needed to do to improve and how to go about this. They were also expected to consider the teacher's comments and their own assessment, and to act on the advice to improve their work.
>
> Ofsted (2008b: 15)

Peer feedback and self-assessment involve learners coming to judgements about what they have achieved and what they need to do to make further progress. It is not as simple as students marking their own maths or that of their peers. Instead, peer- and self-assessment is about getting learners to reflect on the learning process in an evaluative and critical way.

The use of a learning continuum, based on the objectives for the lesson, is an effective way of helping students to be clear about how they can make progress in maths. It allows them to assess where they are in their learning journey and where they need to go. In this way, the emphasis is on the pupils' continuing learning journey over the course of the lesson (or series of lessons), as opposed to believing that they are simply able to 'do' or 'not do' maths. An example follows on page 64.

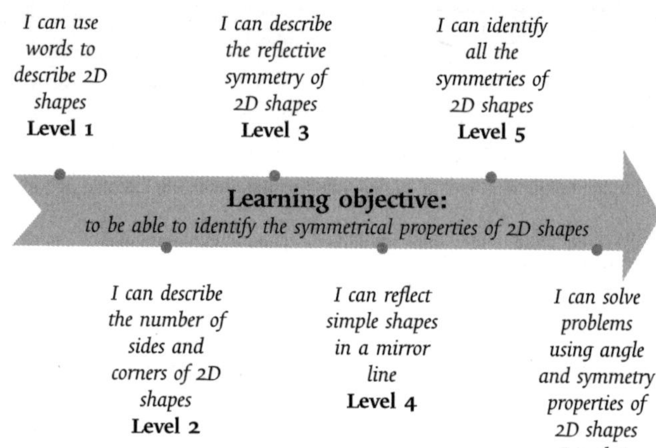


Throughout the lesson, you should steal moments to gather evidence of the progress made by students in the direction of their learning. A mini-plenary, in which students indicate how far they have travelled (perhaps, even, by getting out of their seats and standing against a large-scale continuum), is a great way to assess progress, especially if you have an observer in your classroom.

Because the process of learning is a journey, it is important to remind students to frequently check their own progress in relation to the distance travelled towards the learning outcome. Jackie Beere (2013: 94) describes this as Dedicated Improvement and Reflection Time (DIRT). This means spending quality time in your lesson returning their work, letting them read your comments, soaking in the feedback *and then responding to it*. This may change the way in which you write your feedback: you may set them a little task, correction or extra challenge to be tackled during DIRT. This is a highly effective way of supporting learners in deepening their understanding and strengthening their skills.

Your time is precious, but the traditional response to your marking can simply be a cursory glance at their grade before moving on to the next thing. This form of 'marking and response' means your feedback becomes part of their learning journey and pupils get into the habit of revisiting, reinforcing and reflecting on their learning. It has the added benefit of demonstrating in their books how students are interacting with their work and responding to your feedback – and making progress as a result.

By regularly introducing checkpoints into maths lessons, the quality of reflective self-assessment is enhanced. It also encourages students to focus on the *quality* of their work in relation to the success criteria. These are the times when learners take a moment or two to reread, rework, redraft, check, correct, neaten, amend and improve their work. It gives students more control over, and responsibility for, the outcomes of their learning and makes assessment a transparent and integral part of the learning process.

Feedback that works well during DIRT is commonly less descriptive and more imperative:

> *'Good work! Now try to create three more examples of patterns with a rotational symmetry of order 5.'*

*'Redraft these statements, this time using a fraction, decimal or percentage (instead of words) to describe the probability of the event.'*

*'This is visually confusing. Think about choosing a more appropriate scale and redraw the graph.'*

*'Rework these examples, this time using factorisation to solve the quadratic equation instead of relying on the quadratic formula and your calculator.'*

*'Revisit these questions and give reasons for how you came to your solutions by quoting appropriate angle and/or circle theorems.'*

*'Imagine* $x = -7$ *instead. What would the value of each expression be now? Remember to show your working.'*

*'Go back over your solutions to give the prime factorisation in index form. Why is this a useful thing to do?'*

The important point is that students are actually given time to do it! Responding to feedback is the most powerful way to help them make progress. It also gives you time in the lesson to check that learners are on track and work with those who need extra input to develop their skills, understanding or knowledge.

Dedicated Improvement and Reflection Time can be managed individually or in pairs. When peer-assessing, encourage students to use sentence starters such as 'what went well' and 'even better if'. This focuses comments on areas of strength and areas for development in a supportive and constructive way. Effective peer- and self-assessment is predicated on an understanding of what the 'perfect' answer looks like. It can be helpful, therefore, to provide students with a model answer or success criteria before they attempt to assess their work.

For example, when drawing a bar graph the following checklist can be used:

### Drawing a bar graph: success criteria

- Is there a title that explains what the graph is showing?
- Do both axes have labels?
- Does the y-axis have equally spaced values?
- Does the y-axis have a sensible scale?
- Are the bars of equal width?
- Are there spaces between each bar?
- Are the spaces of equal width?
- Is the graph large enough such that it can be clearly read?
- Do the bar heights match the data accurately?
- Has a ruler been used to draw all lines?

In addition to checklists such as this, you may also wish to provide some prompts for learners to use as they peer- or self-assess:

- This is the best method because ...

- You have met the criteria here by ...
- This is your best answer because ...
- You have made an error here by ...
- You have misunderstood this concept because ...
- To move on to the next level you need to ...
- What would happen if ...?
- A better method would be ...
- You could work more efficiently by ...
- Your answer is in the wrong form because ...
- You need to simplify your answer by ...
- You have introduced error into your calculation by ...

During the perfect maths lesson, teachers need to assess student progress at every opportunity. This may be achieved through effective questioning (see Chapter 2), discussion and observation. It is important that, even in the final throes of your lesson, you assess progress by bringing the lesson to a clear close. A widely used strategy for gaining a snapshot of understanding at the very end of the lesson is to use traffic lights, where red means, 'I do not understand ... yet', amber means, 'I am beginning to understand and need more practice', and green means, 'I understand and I am confident to move on'. Depending on your class, you may wish to assess understanding in this way by:

- A show of hands.
- Use of a traffic light 'fan' or flashcards.
- Thumbs up/to the side/down.

- Handing books into a red, amber or green basket (the promise of some extra special attention for the red books when marking will encourage those who really struggled to be honest about it).
- Sticky notes or exit cards.[2]

The following tried and tested activities are very helpful when it comes to effectively assessing progress in maths lessons (and can make great plenaries).

## Pass the exam[3]

Based on the party game 'pass the parcel', the teacher prepares by enclosing a small gift in copious layers of wrapping paper. Between each layer is a question based on the topic that has been studied. Music is played and, when it stops, the person holding the parcel must unwrap it, read aloud the question and provide an answer. To keep everybody's attention, point out that all of the questions will feature on next week's class test!

## Give me five

Students are asked to provide five examples of things they have learned in the lesson, things they have enjoyed or things they have not yet understood. For example, 'Give me

---

2 Didau (2012: 120) suggests including the following prompts on sticky notes or exit cards: ▲ This point is really clear, ■ One thing that squares with things I already know is ... and ● An idea that is still going round in my head is ...

3 This idea has been adapted from Keeling (2009: 34).

five fractions equivalent to two-thirds' or, 'Give me five fractions that add up to 1'.

## Odd one out

Students identify the odd one out by applying knowledge gained during the lesson. You can gauge the depth of pupil understanding better by ensuring that there is no one 'correct' answer. For example, find the odd one out from the following:

| Rhombus | Equilateral triangle | Square | Kite |
|---|---|---|---|

Answers might include the equilateral triangle because the other shapes are all quadrilaterals or the kite because the other shapes have all sides equal. Students should be encouraged to think outside the box – for example, choosing the square because it is the only shape which could never have an interior angle of 60°.

## Coin toss[4]

Students prepare for a test in pairs, supporting and challenging one another to ensure that they both understand the topic as fully as possible. After, say, 15 minutes of preparation

4 This idea has been adapted from Keeling (2009: 126).

time each pair flips a coin. The 'loser' has to sit the test but both pupils share the mark!

## Call my bluff

Three students are selected to each read aloud a statement linked to the learning objectives of the lesson. Only one of these pupils is reading a correct statement and the rest of the class must determine who the truth-teller is. For example:

| The area of a circle is given by pi times diameter | The area of a circle is given by pi times diameter squared | The area of a circle is given by pi times radius squared |
|---|---|---|

## Who wants to be a mathionaire?

Based on the television quiz show *Who Wants to Be a Millionaire?*, the teacher prepares a series of multiple-choice questions of increasing difficulty linked to the learning objectives of the lesson. Students can play along using mini-whiteboards to reveal their answers. Lifelines can include ask your partner, a class vote or ask the teacher! A quick internet search will save time as there are plenty of free online versions you can use.

## Checklist: assessment of, for and as learning in maths lessons

- Share clear learning objectives at the start of every lesson, using a learning continuum where appropriate. ☑
- Focus oral feedback by giving 'a medal and a mission'. ☑
- Avoid 'ticking and flicking' – reserve your time for providing expert advice and guidance. ☑
- Regularly afford students Dedicated Improvement and Reflection Time (DIRT) so they can respond to your feedback with action that embeds and displays their progress. ☑
- Provide regular opportunities to read the work of others and comment on the mathematics used. ☑
- Scrutinise books regularly and see if you can detect how pupils are responding to your feedback and thereby making progress over time. ☑
- Use 'what went well' and 'even better if' to structure self- and peer-assessment. ☑
- Ensure feedback is a two-way process between teacher and student – you are a learner too! ☑

## Chapter 5

# Relationships for Learning in Maths Lessons

Children are, essentially, emotional beings (see Morris 2009: 78). Notice, for example, that pupils will ask one another, '*Who* have you got today?' as opposed to, '*What* have you got today?' For young people, it is not so much about what they learn in maths but rather how maths makes them *feel*. This leads to some interesting questions for maths teachers. When planning your lessons do you think about how you want learners to feel during each learning episode? How will you excite and intrigue them? How will you challenge them without undermining their self-confidence? How will you use humour to create the right neurochemical state for autonomic learning? These are important questions for teachers who want to deliver the perfect maths lesson. After all, as paediatric neurologist and Independent Thinking associate Andrew Curran says, 'If your heart's not engaged then your head don't work' (quoted in Keeling, 2006: 6).

If children feel loved and understood their self-esteem is increased, leading to an improvement in self-confidence which, in turn, engages the learner emotionally with their learning. This is the best possible environment in which anyone can learn (see Curran, 2008: 128). The challenge for maths teachers is to help pupils enjoy their maths lessons (even if it isn't their favourite subject) because positive emotions are essential for learning. The best way to do this as a maths teacher is to believe that you are a powerful factor in delivering outstanding learning and capable of doing just that! According to John Hattie (2009: 162), the conviction that you are a 'change agent', that you can make a difference because you believe that the outcomes for all children are not fixed, but influenced by you, is crucial to successful teaching.

In his book, *Emotional Intelligence*, Daniel Goleman (1996: 95) outlines the power of emotions in facilitating thinking. He explains that, by channelling our emotions, we are more able to rein in impulses, regulate our mood, delay gratification and motivate ourselves to persist with the result that we become better learners. For maths teachers, all of this means that when children feel *safe and secure* they are able to take risks and apply existing mathematical knowledge to unknown situations. When children feel *confident and encouraged* they are able to wrestle with the general and the abstract. When children feel *capable and taken notice of* they are able to think independently and link ideas to previous learning. In other words, when your classroom is characterised by a climate of emotional intelligence, children become better at maths. It's as simple (and as difficult) as that.

Hywel Roberts (2012: 28) describes emotional intelligence as demonstrating empathy, listening well, controlling your emotions and understanding the make-up of the school you work in (its positive and negative aspects). The emotionally intelligent classroom differs from conventional classrooms because emotions are a sign of strength, not weakness. In the emotionally intelligent classroom, emotions spark creativity and support good judgement; they do not undermine authority or act as a barrier to control. Too often emotions have no place in maths lessons and, consequently, too often young people regard maths as boring and irrelevant. However, emotional awareness and management are the essential levers to creating the optimum neurochemical state for learning (and, therefore, the key to getting 'good' grades).

Dopamine is the number one, learning-related, memory-boosting neurochemical – and a teacher's best friend. Managing the emotional climate of your classroom to produce the right levels of dopamine in learners' brains means that they will have no choice but to learn, whether they want to or not (see Gilbert, 2011: 82)! The most effective means of achieving this is through reward or the anticipation of reward. In a maths lesson, rewards might include:

- A joke
- Opportunities for movement
- Group work
- A puzzle
- Team work

- A giggle
- A game
- Listening to music
- A novelty
- A curiosity or surprise

Here are a few curiosities to baffle and intrigue your students:[1]

- What gets bigger the more you take away from it?
- What is special about this square?

| | | | |
|---|---|---|---|
| 16 | 3 | 2 | 13 |
| 5 | 10 | 11 | 8 |
| 9 | 6 | 7 | 12 |
| 4 | 15 | 14 | 1 |

- How long would it take you to count to one billion, if you counted at a rate of one per second, and did not take any breaks?

1 These ideas have been adapted from McFall (2013: 171, 188, 194–195).

And here are a few silly examples to get the kids giggling:[2]

- Have you heard my maths chat-up line? 'Hey baby, I don't mean to be obtuse, but you are acute girl.' Works every time!
- I hired an odd-job man to do eight jobs for me. When I got back, he'd only done jobs 1, 3, 5 and 7.
- Why did the mutually exclusive events break up? They had nothing in common.
- Have you heard about the mathematical plant? It has square roots.
- Last night I dreamed that I was weightless! I was like, 0mg.
- Why did the chicken cross the Möbius strip? To get to the same side.

Silly, yes, but very much key to getting children in the right state of mind for learning. Better still, the anticipation of reward means that, simply on approaching your classroom and seeing you smiling at the door, the optimal neurochemical state for learning is created before your lesson even begins because the learner knows that your classroom is where 'the good stuff happens'.

The elevation of mathematics to a position of superiority in schools has had the unintentional consequence of damaging maths education for children. Why? Because children are

2 Many of these are the result of spending too much time on Twitter (the best free CPD a teacher can get)!

afraid. They are afraid of making mistakes, of not knowing what to do and of failure. This fear is amplified in the maths classroom because children believe that, above all other subjects, failure in maths is the worst of all failures. In the perfect maths lesson, then, the teacher must obviate the fear of failure. Indeed, we must encourage students to fail better!

> The most skilful teachers were able to adapt their lessons on the basis of the information they gathered. Sometimes this involved giving specific support to pupils who were struggling, or an extra challenge to those finding the work easy. On other occasions, it involved bringing the whole class together to deal with a common difficulty or to allow pupils to share their ideas. Wrong answers were welcomed as an opportunity to explore how a misconception had arisen. Pupils did not fear making mistakes as they too recognised how unravelling an error helped their understanding.
>
> Ofsted (2012a: 23–24)

One of the best ways to mitigate a fear of failure is to show children that we admire hard work and that the best learning is learning from mistakes we have made. Some of the most useful phrases include:

*'If this is making your brain hurt, it means we're learning.'*

*'Have you found today's lesson difficult? Got stuck? Made mistakes? Good! It was worth coming.'*

*'Has anyone made an interesting mistake they could share with the class to help us all learn?'*

*'That's not correct but you've helped to highlight an important misconception that will make us all better at maths. Thanks!'*

*'You're going to love this – it's really challenging.'*

*'Which part did you struggle most with? Can you tell us how you got yourself unstuck?'*

*'You didn't get that right but you kept trying and learned from your mistakes. That makes you a brilliant learner.'*

*'Some of you have found this lesson difficult but that's good because we can learn why, sort it out and get you making great progress.'*

This type of thinking is described by Carol Dweck (2006: 19–20) as a growth mindset. Children with a growth mindset believe that their talents and skills can be developed through hard work and effort. Children with a 'fixed' mindset, on the other hand, believe that their intelligence is a fixed trait and consequently they are less likely to engage in challenging opportunities for mathematical thinking.

Consider the differences between the characteristics of a fixed and growth mindset, and the implications for learners in your classroom. For example, if students believe that intelligence is a fixed trait – you have a certain amount of it and that's that – they will worry about how much intelligence they have and will be interested in looking and feeling as if they have enough. Conversely, if students believe that intelligence is something that can be increased through one's own effort, they will be keen to work hard and learn as much as they can. Children with a fixed mindset will withdraw from learning opportunities in your classroom because they don't want their inadequacies to be revealed. However, children with a growth mindset will throw themselves into difficult tasks in order to learn something new. Children with a fixed mindset need easy successes to feel clever, whereas those with a growth mindset are excited by challenge (Clarke, 2008: 19–20).

A simple classroom display, making use of the phrases below, can begin the process of changing mindsets (yours and theirs):

- If you hear yourself thinking, 'I can't do this' tell yourself, 'I can't do this yet.'
- If you hear yourself thinking, 'I'm no good at this' tell yourself, 'I can become better at this.'
- If you hear yourself thinking, 'What grade did I get?' ask instead, 'What can I do to improve?'

However, change can be difficult. When pupils (or teachers) hold on to a fixed mindset it is because, at some point in their lives, it has served a good purpose for them (Dweck, 2006: 224). The fixed mindset can be a source of security, confidence and self-esteem. Asking people to change their mindset means facing up to all the things that have appeared threatening in the past, such as challenge, criticism and set-backs. But change it we must if we are to achieve our utmost influence, capability and individuality.

With the very best of intentions, maths teachers can be guilty of reinforcing the characteristics of a fixed mindset. Students who have received poor test grades, for example, are sometimes reassured that maths just isn't 'their thing' and that they are talented in 'other ways'. Of course, teachers of the perfect maths lesson must instead convey a growth mindset to students by using language carefully and communicating praise with purpose.

When giving praise, it is important to avoid praising the person by referring to their intelligence or talent. Likewise, a focus should not be given to praising the outcome of their learning (the 'final product' if you will). In so doing, maths teachers risk reinforcing students' belief that their ability is fixed. Phrases to avoid include:

*'Perfect score – you're a natural!'*

*'You're so smart.'*

*'Brilliant – you did that really quickly.'*

*'Fantastic – you didn't make any mistakes!'*

*'Great answer – I can always rely on you.'*

Such comments will lead to the avoidance of challenging tasks for some learners, allowing the 'clever' kids to keep on looking clever and the 'dumb' kids to keep on feeling dumb. Instead, a growth mindset is promoted by focusing praise on the process of learning by referring to effort, resilience and improvement. This ensures that children do not lose confidence or motivation when the going gets tough:

*'I like the way you found a different method for solving that problem. Can you teach it to the rest of the class?'*

*'You've worked really hard on this problem. What do you need to do to move on to the next level?'*

*'Well done for persevering. Tell me what you've learned so far.'*

*'What can you do now that you couldn't do before?'*

*'Last lesson you were so determined. Let's see if you can find some of that motivation and apply it to this problem.'*

*'I like that you've tried the most difficult questions. That will really help you to learn.'*

*'You cleared your mind of "can't" and really got stuck into that. Well done.'*

Of course, we are teachers of children before we are teachers of mathematics. And the most powerful praise to link children emotionally with their learning includes, simply, smiles, 'thank yous' and 'well dones'. You can't go wrong by remembering that praise should always be:

- Personal
- Sensitive
- Linked to learning
- Sincere

- Specific
- Proportionate

Rewarding effort rather than outcome is a simple way of reminding your pupils that what matters is how hard they are working rather than the grade or mark they achieve. This is especially important in an educational world driven by exam grades and levels. Carol Dweck's (2006) advice for teachers and parents is to reward the effort and focus on the process of the *learning journey* to develop a growth mindset that is resilient and leads to a love of learning.

> [In outstanding lessons] pupils consistently display a thirst for knowledge and a love of learning, including in independent, group and whole class work, which have a very strong impact on their progress in lessons.
>
> Ofsted (2014: 44)

By following the advice in this book, children should learn to love your maths lessons. And, as a result, students will behave better because effective teaching is the basis for good discipline. However, from time to time things will go wrong in your classroom: we're dealing with children, after all! It is helpful for teachers to understand why children (and, in particular, adolescents) can find it difficult to manage their emotions, leading to unpredictable behaviour, which brings us back to the brain.

When the sensory system in the thalamus detects a threat to survival (for example, a maths teacher raising their voice or towering over a student) it sends a mental impression of the perceived threat to two places: the amygdala and the pre-frontal cortex. The amygdala forms part of the limbic system – the emotion and memory centre of the brain. Its job is to provoke a physical response to the threat – for example, releasing catecholamines (such as adrenaline) into the bloodstream, widening the eyes, clenching the fists and preparing muscles in the legs and arms for action. The pre-frontal cortex, on the other hand, is responsible for dealing with emotions *intelligently* and allows us to manage and influence our feelings (see Morris 2009: 76–78). The problem? Although the sensory and limbic systems develop during childhood, the pre-frontal cortex does not mature until adulthood. Children's reaction processes therefore tend to be driven by the amygdala in a way that bypasses their 'rational brain'.

For maths teachers, this means that when a pupil becomes highly agitated in the classroom we need to give them the space and the time needed for their 'rational brain' to regain control. In his book, *Why Do I Need A Teacher When I've Got Google?* (2011: 78), Ian Gilbert provides a framework for achieving this, neatly wrapped up in the acronym STAR:

**S***top*
**T***hink*
**A***ct*
**R***eflect*

When it comes to behaviour in the classroom, prevention is better than cure. Maths teachers can minimise opportunities for unwanted behaviour by following this very simple advice:

- Arrange seats appropriately before the lesson.
- Ensure the lesson starts promptly.
- Stand prominently in the room.
- Make eye contact with the students.
- Ensure that there are no unplanned breaks in the learning.
- Enhance meaning with vocal variation reinforced with movement.
- Sharpen the learning objectives.

During the lesson, classroom control is often lost at those times when students are required to move from one learning episode to another. Learning to manage a smooth transition is one of the most important skills a teacher should master, so before attempting to change the direction of the lesson, you should ensure that every pupil is silent and looking at you (see Beadle, 2010: 19).

Maths teachers can manage transitions more effectively by using the acronym PRINT when giving instructions to a class:[3]

---

3 A useful tool advocated by Dr Geoff Moss, a leading trainer in Assertive Discipline®.

**P***urpose*

**R***esources*

**I***n or out of seat*

**N***oise*

**T***ime*

For example, 'Year 7, we are now going to practise algebraic substitution by completing a diamond rank. All you require to do this is the set of cards in the envelope on your table. I need you to stay in your seats and I need you to use your partner voice. You have 11-and-a-half minutes to complete the task.'

Notice that the purpose of the task is focused and has been linked to the learning objectives of the lesson. The resources have been prepared and deployed in advance of the learning. The expectations of student movement and volume have been explicitly stated. The timescale is specific and creates a sense of urgency (try to avoid setting 'conventional' time limits of 5 or 10 minutes). Finally, the instructions should be repeated. Building this routine into your behaviour management toolkit will keep your lessons running smoothly, and reinforcing the routine offers an opportunity to recognise the contribution of the majority of children who are doing what is expected of them (see Hook and Vass, 2004: 116).

> Pupils' attitudes, behaviour and achievement are best where staff know pupils well and plan lessons which are well matched to their abilities and interests and take account of their different learning styles. In these lessons the transition between activities is managed well.
>
> Ofsted (2005: 15)

However hard we may try to prevent misbehaviour, children will always find opportunities to be silly, call out, swing on chairs, chat, whisper, ignore instructions, disrupt and generally irritate their teacher, who has worked hard to prepare a great lesson for them. The following tried and tested strategies are especially useful when it comes to managing behaviour in maths lessons:

- Don't overreact – after all, they're kids! Keep your cool and don't take it personally if a child misbehaves in your lesson. Just draw very firm, consistent boundaries which clearly reflect your expectations.
- Be assertive – ensure instructions are concise, clear and non-negotiable ('I need you to be silent now, thank you').
- Provide a sense of choice – gain control of your classroom by first giving a little away. If a child is misbehaving, offer them a compromise so that they can comply without losing face ('I need you to either put your phone in your bag or on my desk'). This is the most powerful method for avoiding confrontation in the

classroom and makes the student responsible for sorting out their own behaviour (see Cowley, 2009: 37).

- 'Tactically tackle' unwanted or disruptive behaviour – for example, if a child is whispering when they shouldn't be, simply move closer to them until they stop.
- Catch them being good – focus your comments on those children who are following instructions. Attention-seekers will soon realise that good behaviour is the best way to get a response from you.
- Partially agree – try to find a middle ground when reprimanding a student ('I accept that you were talking about your work but at the moment I need you to be silent').
- Then – make compromises by introducing a condition to you instructions ('When you sit back in your chair then I will look at your work').
- Get them into routines – how you design your classroom routines is less important than ensuring that you stick to them. Children like to know where they stand with a teacher.
- Expect compliance – use 'thank you' instead of 'please' when you give an instruction to create a sense of obligation to comply ('I need you to put your pen down now, thank you').
- Laugh – relieve tension in the classroom with humour or even just a smile!
- Defer sanctions – if you need to sanction a child do it privately and, if possible, after the lesson.

> [In outstanding lessons] skilled and highly consistent behaviour management by all staff makes a strong contribution to an exceptionally positive climate for learning.
>
> Ofsted (2014: 44)

Remember, there is a world beyond the four walls of your classroom so try to retain a sense of perspective. And, above all else, have fun. An awful lot of fun! As award-winning educational author and founder of Independent Thinking, Ian Gilbert, says, 'Life, like education, is too important to be taken seriously' (2014: 26).

## Checklist: relationships for learning in maths lessons

- Believe in your mission – outcomes for children are not fixed but influenced by you. ☑
- Get them in the right state for learning by telling a joke, listening to music, surprising or puzzling them! ☑
- Use language to help children to 'fail better' and learn from their mistakes. ☑
- Promote a growth mindset by giving praise responsibly. Praise effort and help them to focus on the journey, not just the outcome. ☑

- Understand how the brain reacts to the challenges maths presents. ☑
- Help children to Stop, Think, Act, Reflect. ☑
- Manage transitions using PRINT. ☑
- Have fun – maths is too important to be taken seriously. ☑

# Chapter 6
# The Perfect Maths Lesson Self-Assessment

In reading this book, you've shown a commitment to being the very best maths teacher you can be. Not for Ofsted or the senior leadership team but for the children you teach every day. In helping them to achieve you, too, will need to adapt, reflect and self-evaluate to ensure that you are always improving your craft. This self-assessment tool is handy for celebrating areas of strength and highlighting those areas that still need development, with a particular focus on engagement, challenge, independence, assessment and relationships. Complete it honestly by adopting a 'best fit' approach, taking into account a series of lessons over, for example, one school term.[1]

1 Adapted from Beere (2013: 130). Source attributed to Bridgnorth Endowed School, Shropshire.

| Engagement | Inadequate | Requires improvement | Good | Outstanding |
| --- | --- | --- | --- | --- |
| **The start of the lesson** | Few pupils hooked into learning. Lesson takes too long to begin. | Some pupils hooked into learning. Lesson starts promptly. | A purposeful start to the lesson with most pupils hooked into learning. | All pupils immediately hooked into learning with little input from the teacher. |
| **Pace** | Pace does not vary and the teacher does not respond to pupils' difficulties. Some periods of inactivity. | Pace varies according to level of difficulty. However, interventions are too often unsuccessful. | Pace varies according to level of difficulty allowing most pupils to make progress. | A clear sense of pace which varies according to feedback from pupils allowing all to make progress. |
| **Focus** | A lack of variation in activities leads to too many pupils losing focus. Pupils are not involved in their learning for | A lack of variation in activities leads to some pupils losing focus. There are some periods in which pupils are | A good range of activities keep most pupils on task throughout the lesson. | An imaginative range of activities keep all pupils on task throughout the lesson. |

| | | | | |
|---|---|---|---|---|
| | significant periods. | not actively learning. | | |
| **Relevance** | Learning outcomes are not relevant and do not link to previous learning experiences. | Learning outcomes are linked to previous learning but pupils do not identify with the aims of the lesson. | Learning outcomes are relevant and draw on previous learning experiences. | Learning outcomes are highly relevant, linked to pupils' lives and connected to previous learning experiences. |
| **Lesson structure** | Mostly teacher-led with little input from pupils. Lesson structure is inflexible. | Mostly teacher-led with little input from pupils. Lesson structure has some flexibility. | Pupils play an active role in their learning. Lesson structure is flexible in response to pupils' needs. | Teacher and pupils lead learning. Lesson structure is highly flexible and constantly responds to pupils' needs. |

| Challenge | Mostly inadequate | Mostly requires improvement | Mostly good | Mostly outstanding |
|---|---|---|---|---|
| **Subject knowledge** | Teacher's subject knowledge is insecure leading to poor development of mathematical skills. | Teacher's subject knowledge is reasonably secure leading to some development of mathematical skills. | Teacher's subject knowledge is sound leading to good development of mathematical skills. | Teacher's subject knowledge is outstanding leading to excellent development of mathematical skills. |
| **Questioning** | Limited, closed teacher-led questioning restricted to a few pupils. No use of questions to assess pupil progress. | Frequent but often closed teacher-led questioning. Pupil progress is not adequately assessed through questions. | Frequent, open teacher-led questions with adequate thinking time. Questions uncover misconceptions. Questions invited from pupils. | Teacher questioning challenges pupils and encourages metacognition. All pupils involved in asking their own questions to deepen understanding. |
| **Differentiation** | Pupil groups not identified and teaching fails to | Pupil groups identified and teacher responds to | Pupil groups identified and high expectations of | Carefully designed, personalised activities challenge |

| | | | | |
|---|---|---|---|---|
| | cater for individual needs. | individual needs during lesson. | individuals communicated through effectively adapted tasks. | all pupil groups, including the most able and most vulnerable. |
| **Learning support** | Learning support assistants are not included in planning. They complete work for pupils. | Learning support assistants help pupils to complete work but do not necessarily support learning. | Learning support assistants understand the aims of the lesson and provide appropriate strategies for pupils. | Learning support assistants are actively involved in planning and teach necessary skills to pupils leading to improved progress. |
| **Conceptual understanding** | Lesson relies on rote learning without explaining mathematical concepts. | Lesson focuses on procedural knowledge and routine without explaining mathematical concepts sufficiently. | Most pupils develop conceptual understanding leading to procedural knowledge with significant teacher input. | All pupils develop conceptual understanding leading to procedural knowledge. |

| Independence | Mostly inadequate | Mostly requires improvement | Mostly good | Mostly outstanding |
|---|---|---|---|---|
| **Grouping and roles** | Pupil groupings are, at best, ad hoc and do not lead to any progress in learning. | Pupils are grouped but in an unplanned way with no self-regulation of learning. | Pupils are grouped in a planned way with some self-regulation of learning. | Pupils are grouped in a planned way and self-regulate their own learning by fulfilling roles effectively. |
| **Resources** | A lack of learning resources impedes progress. | Learning resources are available but not obviously so. | Learning resources are readily available but pupils do not use them without prompting from the teacher. | Learning resources are readily available and pupils know how to use them well. |
| **Self-regulation** | Pupils are shown how to solve mathematical problems by the teacher. | Pupils are involved, through class discussion, in developing a shared approach to solving mathematical problems. | Pupils are given some choice about how to tackle mathematical problems. | Pupils are able to approach mathematical problems in a variety of ways and develop their own strategies for solving them. |

| | | | | |
|---|---|---|---|---|
| **Homework** | Its purpose is unclear and pupil responses are erratic. | Its purpose is clear but lacks challenge. | Its purpose is closely linked to learning outcomes and engages pupils. | Its purpose is linked explicitly to learning outcomes and clearly assesses progress towards them. It is challenging and extends learning. |
| **Numeracy and literacy** | Opportunities to develop numeracy and literacy skills are missed. | Opportunities to develop numeracy and literacy skills are present but their importance is not highlighted to pupils. | Opportunities to develop numeracy and literacy skills are frequent and highlighted for their importance. | Opportunities to develop numeracy and literacy skills pervade the lesson and students engage readily in them. |

| Assessment | Mostly inadequate | Mostly requires improvement | Mostly good | Mostly outstanding |
|---|---|---|---|---|
| **Learning outcomes** | Not shared. Unrealistically high or low. | Shared with some sense of context. May not represent an appropriate level of challenge. | Shared with a clear sense of purpose. Realistically challenging. | Well-planned outcomes are shared, challenging and used throughout the lesson to assess progress. |
| **Oral feedback** | General, sporadic oral feedback which does not help pupils to make progress in their learning. | Oral feedback is more focused and helps some pupils to make progress. | Oral feedback is focused and specific helping most pupils to make good progress. | Highly focused and specific oral feedback pervades the lesson and helps all pupils to make excellent progress. |
| **Written feedback** | Written feedback is not useful and does not explain clearly what needs to be done to | Written feedback is useful but lacks specificity. Pupils do not respond readily to feedback. | Written feedback clearly identifies strengths and areas for development with clear targets | Written feedback explains clearly what learners need to do to improve. Pupils respond |

| | | | | |
|---|---|---|---|---|
| | improve. | | for improvement. Some evidence of pupils responding to this. | readily to feedback and make progress as a result. |
| **Self- and peer-assessment** | Pupils do not assess learning against outcomes. | Pupils assess learning in a general and supportive way but this does not lead to progress over time. | Pupils assess learning regularly and accurately against outcomes. | Pupils assess learning effectively and with insight. Use of success criteria leads to progress over time. |
| **Progress** | Little or no progress towards outcomes is made by too many pupils. | Good progress is made by most pupils and most are clear about how to address gaps. | Good progress is made by all pupils and all are clear about how to address gaps. | Rapid and sustained progress is made by all pupils and this is rigorously evidenced in the lesson and in books. |

| Relationships | Mostly inadequate | Mostly requires improvement | Mostly good | Mostly outstanding |
|---|---|---|---|---|
| **Classroom climate** | The classroom is not a friendly place to be and pupils lack the confidence needed to engage fully in their learning. | The classroom is a friendly and safe place to be. Too few pupils feel confident enough to take risks in their learning. | The classroom is a friendly and safe place to be and pupils feel confident to take risks in their learning. | The classroom is characterised by emotional intelligence and pupils feel safe, confident, encouraged and capable. |
| **Promoting a growth mindset** | The language used by the teacher reinforces pupils' belief that their ability is fixed. | The language used by the teacher promotes hard work and effort. Mistakes are not shared or used to support learning. | The language used by the teacher promotes hard work and effort. Mistakes are celebrated and shared. | The language used by the teacher encourages pupils to be hardworking, resilient and inquisitive. |
| **Praise** | Praise is rarely given and pupils do not feel encouraged. | Praise is given frequently but is general and does not relate to the | Regular praise is personal, specific and relates to the learning journey | Praise is personal, specific, sincere and linked explicitly to the |

| | | | | |
|---|---|---|---|---|
| | | learning journey and effort. | and effort. | process to create a growth mindset. |
| **Transitions** | Transitions are uncontrolled and haphazard. There are too many breaks in the learning. | Transitions are controlled but lead to some breaks in the learning. | Transitions are managed very well leading to no breaks in the learning. | Transitions are managed highly effectively leading to no breaks in the learning and all pupils staying on task. |
| **Behaviour for learning** | Persistent low-level disruption or rudeness leads to incomplete work. | Some low-level disruption is present and it is over-managed. | Very little disruption is present and it is managed subtly and expertly. | Teaching has cultured pupils who are habitually enthusiastic and cooperative. |

|  | Mostly inadequate | Mostly requires improvement | Mostly good | Mostly outstanding |
|---|---|---|---|---|
| **Complete your action plan:** | | | | |
|  | | | | |

# The Perfect Maths Lesson Ultimate Checklist

## Engaging learners in maths lessons

- Use a short, snappy activity to set the scene and 'hook' learners into the learning. ☑
- Vary the pace of each learning episode. ☑
- Provide space for reflection and for asking questions. ☑
- Break up long periods of stationary learning with movement. ☑
- Use time limits to keep learning focused. ☑
- Prepare and deploy resources in advance of the lesson. ☑
- Minimise teacher-talk. ☑
- Link the learning to students' own lives. ☑

## Challenging learners in maths lessons

- Ensure questions focus thinking on the key concepts. ☑
- Use open questions. ☑

- Provide thinking time. ☑
- Avoid hands up. ☑
- Use pose, pause, pounce, bounce. ☑
- Ask students to summarise one another's thinking. ☑
- Provide key words and word banks for written response questions. ☑
- Sensitively design different tasks for different pupils (with the same learning objective). ☑
- Make good use of learning support assistants. ☑
- Underpin procedural knowledge with conceptual understanding. ☑
- Let students teach one another (or younger students). ☑

## Independent learning in maths lessons

- Make learning objectives explicit at the start of the lesson. ☑
- Ensure the lesson plan is flexible enough for students to determine the direction their learning takes. ☑
- Build in opportunities for reflection during the lesson. ☑
- Provide students with choices about their learning during the lesson. ☑
- Hold learners accountable for their learning (they should be working harder than you). ☑

- Organise pupils carefully into groups, assigning roles if necessary. ☑
- Ensure learning resources are available for students to call on. ☑
- Introduce a 'stuck cycle'. ☑
- Rein in your impulse to answer questions. ☑
- Set purposeful homework that challenges and engages. ☑

## Assessment of, for and as learning in maths lessons

- Plan what will be assessed and why. ☑
- Plan the most appropriate assessment method. ☑
- Decide how you will use information from assessments (e.g. will you need to change the course of the learning mid-lesson?). ☑
- Ask learners what they already know about the topic. ☑
- Provide regular opportunities for students to mark their own work and that of others. ☑
- Provide regular opportunities for students to read the work of others and comment on the mathematics used. ☑
- Focus oral feedback using 'a medal and a mission'. ☑
- Focus written feedback by giving clear direction for how to improve, linked to the learning objectives. ☑
- Focus self- and peer-assessment using 'what went well' and 'even better if'. ☑

- Regularly provide Dedicated Improvement and Reflection Time (DIRT). ☑
- Scrutinise books to ensure students are responding to feedback. ☑
- Encourage students to devise their own questions. ☑
- Explain levels and grades in simple language. ☑
- Ensure feedback is a two-way process between teacher and pupil. ☑

## Relationships for learning in maths lessons

- Plan for the heart as well as the head. ☑
- Characterise your classroom by a climate of emotional intelligence. ☑
- Provide 'rewards' such as a joke, curiosity, game or surprise. ☑
- Use language to encourage a mathematical growth mindset. ☑
- Focus praise on effort, resilience and improvements made. ☑
- Ensure praise is personal, sincere and linked to the learning. ☑
- Arrange seats before the lesson and ensure the lesson starts promptly. ☑
- Introduce classroom routines and stick to them. ☑
- Manage transitions between learning episodes using PRINT. ☑

- Encourage students to Stop, Think, Act and Reflect. ☑
- Relieve tension with humour. ☑

## And finally ...

- Smile! Maths education is too important to be taken seriously! ☑

# References and Further Reading


Baker, K. (2007). *The Paideia Proposal: An Educational Manifesto.* New York: Collier Books.

Beadle, P. (2010). *How to Teach.* Carmarthen: Crown House Publishing.

Beere, J. (2012a). *The Perfect (Ofsted) Inspection.* Carmarthen: Independent Thinking Press.

Beere, J. (2012b). *The Perfect (Ofsted) Lesson* (rev. edn). Carmarthen: Crown House Publishing.

Beere, J. (2013). *The Perfect Teacher.* Carmarthen: Crown House Publishing.

Black, P. and Wiliam, D, (1998). Assessment and classroom learning, *Assessment in Education: Principles, Policy and Practice* 5(1): 7–74.

Boaler, J. (2009). *The Elephant in the Classroom.* London: Souvenir Press.

Chiswick, B., Lee, Y. and Miller, P. (2003). Schooling, literacy, numeracy and labour market success, *Economic Record* 79(245): 165–181.

Clarke, S. (2008). *Active Learning through Formative Assessment.* London: Hodder Education.

Coughlan, S. (2013). Pisa tests: UK stagnates as Shanghai tops league table, *BBC News* (3 December). Available at: <http://www.bbc.co.uk/news/education-25187997>.

Cowley, S. (2009). *How to Survive Your First Year in Teaching.* London: Continuum.

Curran, A. (2008). *The Little Book of Big Stuff about the Brain: The True Story of Your Amazing Brain*. Carmarthen: Crown House Publishing.

Didau, D. (2012). *The Perfect (Ofsted) English Lesson*. Carmarthen: Independent Thinking Press.

Dweck, C. S. (2006). *Mindset: The New Psychology of Success*. New York: Ballantine Books.

Friedman, T. (2006). *The World is Flat: The Globalized World in the Twenty-First Century*. London: Penguin.

Gilbert, I. (2011). *Why Do I Need a Teacher When I've Got Google? The Essential Guide to the Big Issues for Every 21st Century Teacher*. Abingdon: Routledge.

Gilbert, I. (2014). *Independent Thinking*. Carmarthen: Independent Thinking Press.

Ginnis, P. (2002). *The Teacher's Toolkit: Raise Classroom Achievement with Strategies for Every Learner*. Carmarthen: Crown House Publishing.

Goleman, D. (1996). *Emotional Intelligence: Why It Can Matter More Than IQ*. London: Bloomsbury.

Griffith, A. and Burns, M. (2012). *Outstanding Teaching: Engaging Learners*. Carmarthen: Crown House Publishing.

Harrison, C. and Howard, S. (2009). *Inside the Primary Black Box: Assessment for Learning in Primary and Early Years Classrooms*. London: GL Assessment.

Hattie, J. (2009). *Visible Learning: A Synthesis of Over 800 Meta-Analyses Relating to Achievement*. London: Routledge.

Hodgson, D. (2009). *The Little Book of Inspirational Teaching Activities: Bringing NLP into the Classroom*. Carmarthen: Crown House Publishing.

Hook, P. and Vass, A. (2004). *Behaviour Management Pocketbook*. Alresford: Teachers' Pocketbooks.

Keeling, D. (2006). On love, laughter and learning, in I. Gilbert (ed.), *The Big Book of Independent Thinking: Do Things No One Does or Do Things Everyone Does in a Way No One Does*. Carmarthen: Crown House Publishing, pp. 3–26.

Keeling, D. (2009). *Rocket Up Your Class! 101 High Impact Activities to Start, Break and End Lessons*. Carmarthen: Crown House Publishing.

McFall, M. (2013). *A Cabinet of Curiosities: The Little Book of Awe and Wonder*. Carmarthen: Independent Thinking Press.

McGill, R. M. (2013). *100 Ideas for Secondary Teachers: Outstanding Lessons*. London: Bloomsbury Education.

Morris, I. (2009). *Teaching Happiness and Well-Being in Schools*. London: Continuum.

Nuthall, G. (2007). *The Hidden Lives of Learners*. Wellington: New Zealand Council for Educational Research Press.

Ofsted (2005). *Managing Challenging Behaviour*. Ref: 2363. Available at: <http://www.ofsted.gov.uk/resources/managing-challenging-behaviour>.

Ofsted (2008a). *Mathematics: Understanding the Score*. Ref: 070063. Available at: <http://www.ofsted.gov.uk/resources/mathematics-understanding-score>.

Ofsted (2008b). *Assessment for Learning: The Impact of National Strategy Support*. Ref: 070244. Available at: <http://www.ofsted.gov.uk/resources/assessment-for-learning-impact-of-national-strategy-support>.

Ofsted (2012a). *Mathematics: Made to Measure*. Ref: 110159. Available at: <http://www.ofsted.gov.uk/resources/mathematics-made-measure>.

Ofsted (2012b). *Engaging Able Mathematics Students: King Edward VI Camp Hill School for Boys*. Ref: 120114. Available at: <http://www.ofsted.gov.uk/resources/good-practice-resource-engaging-able-mathematics-students-king-edward-vi-camp-hill-school-for-boys>.

Ofsted (2012c). *Loosen Up to Become Outstanding in Mathematics: Allenbourn Middle School*. Ref: 130004. Available at: <http://www.ofsted.gov.uk/resources/good-practice-resource-loosen-become-outstanding-mathematics-allenbourn-middle-school>.

Ofsted (2014). *School Inspection Handbook*. Ref: 120101. Available at: <http://www.ofsted.gov.uk/resources/school-inspection-handbook>.

Pink, D. H. (2005). *A Whole New Mind: Why Right-Brainers Will Rule the Future*. New York: Riverhead.

Rimmer, G. (2006). *Number Freaking: The Surreal Sums Behind Everyday Life*. Cambridge: Icon Books.

Roberts, H. (2012). *Oops! Helping Children Learn Accidentally*. Carmarthen: Independent Thinking Press.

Smith, J. (2010). *The Lazy Teacher's Handbook: How Your Students Learn More When You Teach Less*. Carmarthen: Crown House Publishing.